BRIGHT NOTES

THE SCHOOL FOR WIVES AND OTHER WORKS BY MOLIÈRE

Intelligent Education

Nashville, Tennessee

BRIGHT NOTES: The School for Wives and Other Works
www.BrightNotes.com

No part of this publication may be used or reproduced in any manner whatsoever without written permission, except in the case of brief quotations in critical articles and reviews. For permissions, contact Influence Publishers http://www.influencepublishers.com.

ISBN: 978-1-645424-50-5 (Paperback)
ISBN: 978-1-645424-51-2 (eBook)

Published in accordance with the U.S. Copyright Office Orphan Works and Mass Digitization report of the register of copyrights, June 2015.

Originally published by Monarch Press.
Lawrence Hadfield Klibbe, 1965
2020 Edition published by Influence Publishers.

Interior design by Lapiz Digital Services. Cover Design by Thinkpen Designs.

Printed in the United States of America.

Library of Congress Cataloging-in-Publication Data forthcoming.
Names: Intelligent Education
Title: BRIGHT NOTES: The School for Wives and Other Works
Subject: STU004000 STUDY AIDS / Book Notes

CONTENTS

1)	Introduction to Molière	1
2)	The Play to The Precious Damsels	14
3)	Character Analyses	18
4)	Essay Questions and Answers	20
5)	The Play to The School for Wives	22
6)	Character Analyses	33
7)	Essay Questions and Answers	36
8)	The Play to The Tartuffe	38
9)	Character Analyses	43
10)	Essay Questions and Answers	47
11)	The Play to The Misanthrope	51
12)	Character Analyses	62

13)	Essay Questions and Answers	65
14)	The Play to The Miser	69
15)	Character Analyses	81
16)	Essay Questions and Answers	86
17)	The Play to The Would Be Gentleman	89
18)	Character Analyses	99
19)	Essay Questions and Answers	103
20)	The Play to The Learned Ladies	105
21)	Character Analyses	114
22)	Essay Questions and Answers	118
23)	The Play to The Physician in Spite of Himself	121
24)	Character Analyses	129
25)	Essay Questions and Answers	132
26)	The Play to The Imaginary Invalid	134
27)	Character Analyses	144
28)	Essay Questions and Answers	148
29)	Conclusions	150

30) Criticism 154

31) Bibliography 163

INTRODUCTION TO MOLIÈRE

Jean-Baptiste Poquelin was born in Paris and was baptized on January 15, 1622. Later in life, he used the stage name of Molière. There are few reliable sources about the facts of his life. For example, it is not known when he first took the new name, why he exactly wished to change names, and where he found the word Molière.

EARLY LIFE

Molière was the oldest child of a well-to-do, middle-class Parisian family. His father seems to have been a hard-working, thrifty, and ambitious interior decorator. In 1631 he secured an appointment as a royal upholsterer, which provided him with an opportunity to participate in the court of Louis XIII. Molière's mother died when the boy was only ten years old, and his father remarried a year later. At the age of fifteen, Molière was sent to the College of Clermont, a school run by the Jesuits and attended by the children of rich and noble parents. At this school Molière received a thoroughly classical education and undoubtedly came into contact with the theater for the first time, since the Jesuits encouraged the study of drama. Molière also may have studied law in the city of Orleans somewhat later.

FIRST FAILURES AND FLIGHT

In 1643, at the age of twenty-one, Molière shocked his father when he declared that he did not intend to follow in his parent's footsteps as an upholsterer. He also renounced his right of succession to his father's royal title. Six months later he stunned his father again by forming a theatrical company. "The Illustrious Theater," with Madeleine Béjart as his leading lady, business partner, and mistress. At this time the acting profession was condemned by the Church, and the bourgeoisie or middleclass, to which his family belonged, shunned members of the theater. Nevertheless, Molière's father seems to have helped his son, once the initial shock passed and he saw he could not persuade Molière to change his mind. After touring in the provinces, Molière's company came to Paris at the end of 1644. In Paris, "The Illustrious Theater" proved to be anything but illustrious. The competition of other theatrical groups in the big city resulted in the financial failure of the amateurs. Molière was arrested and imprisoned for debt. Molière's father save his son by paying the money owed. In 1646, with three years of experience in the ways of the world of the theater to his credit, Molière fled to the provinces of France.

YEARS OF EXILE

From 1646 until 1658, Molière wandered throughout France with the remnants of his defeated acting company. Little is definitely known of these years except that they must have been years of financial hardship, with a constant change of living quarters, for Molière. However, he perfected his theatrical genius during these twelve years of wandering. He learned to be actor, director, writer, and jack-of-all-trades in the many details of operating a theater. He also came into contact with people from all walks of life. He was to use all these experiences in his later plays. In 1654 Louis XIV was crowned King of France, and the nation started along the path of great political and cultural power.

RETURN TO PARIS

In 1658 Molière returned to the capital and presented before the young king one of his own minor comedies. Its success was not overwhelming, but complete failure as before did not occur. In 1659 Molière had his first hit, *The Precious Damsels*, which was a bold **satire** on the exaggerated, snobbish manners of wealthy and noble women. By the year 1661 the theatrical company of Molière occupied the best theater in Paris.

SUCCESS

For the next twelve years, until his death, Molière enjoyed success on the stage. These are the years when the lives of Louis XIV and Molière are joined. Without the help of the king, before whom he presented his plays, Molière would not have been able to overcome his rivals and enemies to reach the heights of financial and literary success. The artistic originality of Molière began to be recognized in his play of 1662, *The School for Wives*. He combined the French farce, the Italian commedia dell'arte or improvised art, and contemporary social **satire** to create a new type of comedy.

OPPOSITION

Everything did not go smoothly for Molière during these years. In 1662, he married Armande Béjart, the sister of Madeleine, his old friend from the days of "The Illustrious Theater." The marriage proved to be an unhappy one; this personal tragedy is reflected in several of Molière's plays. Despite the fact that Louis XIV was the godfather for Molière's son in 1664, the dramatist encountered great opposition from the Church, the nobility, and social figures who claimed they had been ridiculed by him on the stage. In 1664, he introduced before the king his most daring and controversial play, Tartuffe. It is a severe criticism of religious hypocrisy. Even Louis XIV could not protect his friend from the attacks of his enemies this time. The king was forced to ban the play, and for five years Molière worked to revise Tartuffe and begged the king to permit its performance. In 1669 it was publicly performed and was highly successful.

FURTHER SUCCESSES

During this five-year battle about Tartuffe, Molière continued to produce hits. In 1666 he wrote perhaps his greatest artistic triumph and probably his most profound work, *The Misanthrope*. He satirized the ambitions of the middle class in *The Miser* (1668) and *The Would-Be Gentleman* (1670). In *The Learned Ladies* (1672), Molière criticized insincerity and pretentiousness in women. At the same time that his social criticism became sharper and wittier, he was writing comedies that were more polished in form and style.

DEATH

His own unhappiness and disillusionments were reflected more and more in the plays. Although Molière won wealth and fame during his residence in Paris, his personal life became more and more tragic. Marital difficulties with his wife, Armande, increased, and the cruel attacks of his opponents began to take their toll on Molière. His health was failing, and the doctors became a source of bitter dramatic material for him. In 1666 he had already written one comedy about the medical profession, *The Physician in Spite of Himself*. In 1673, Molière wrote *The Imaginary Invalid*, a serious comedy about the vicious practices of doctors and the victimizing of a fearful public by quacks. During the fourth performance of this play, Molière, already a very ill man, was stricken by a hemorrhage of the lungs as he played the part of Argan, the dupe of the physicians. He died on the same night, February 17, 1673.

His death showed the talent of the man in several ways. Mortally ill, Molière had to portray an imaginary invalid. He also tried to carry on the best tradition of the theater - "the show must go on" - by continuing to perform until he finished the play. His wife was absent when he died because she was frantically attempting to persuade a priest to come to anoint him. At that time, actors were excommunicated or forbidden to enjoy the rites of the Church. In addition, the ecclesiastical officials, still smarting under the attacks of Tartuffe, refused to permit the burial of Molière in consecrated soil.

Molière's good friend, Louis XIV, finally heard the pleas of the dramatist's wife and allowed the burial in a parish cemetery. However, the funeral had to take place privately at night. There is still doubt as to whether or not Molière was buried in church ground and whether or not the remains taken to the Pantheon, shrine of great Frenchmen in Paris, during the French Revolution, were really those of Molière. Molière's final exit from the stage of life may be summed up best in the words of Lord Morley, the British historian: "The best title of Louis XIV to the recollection of posterity is the protection he extended to Molière."

In 1680 Louis XIV merged the theatrical company of Molière with another group to form the Comédie Française or French National Theater. It is known also as the "House of Molière." For almost three hundred years this theater, financed by the French government, has kept alive the tradition of Molière and the other French classic writers by performing their plays. The enormous popularity of Molière continues to be shown by the fact that his plays are performed regularly and to full houses. Because of his importance in French literature, he has often been called the "Shakespeare of France."

THE AGE OF MOLIÈRE

Age Of Louis XIV

Molière's lifetime (1622-1673) embraces only a fraction of the period known in French and European history as the "Age of Louis XIV." Born in 1638, Louis XIV, after the death of Louis XIII in 1643, was proclaimed king under the regency of Cardinal Mazarin but was not crowned until 1654. In 1661, the young monarch became ruler in fact as well as name by asserting his authority over the nation; until his death in 1715, Louis XIV governed as an absolute autocrat under the doctrine of "I am the State." He was thirty-five years old at the time of Molière's death and was generally popular with the people. He had crushed the nobles and unified the country. The order and stability thus achieved appealed to all social classes. Under able ministers like Colbert, Louis XIV employed French energies, diverted from wasteful civil wars and bad administration, in the creation of the dominant power on the European continent. Spain, after the defeat of the Armada by the English in 1688, had gone into decline, and England still had not created an empire with which to assert its growing strength. Thus, given the support of his people, a rich and flourishing economy, and a central government, Louis XIV chose to encourage any enterprise which would boost French prestige and glory.

In the first place, he spent large sums of money on wars to gain military supremacy for France. The nation was opposed by alliances of the other European powers and gradually Louis XIV was checked in his territorial aims. However, he had some successes. For example, in 1700, he named his grandson king of Spain after the death of Charles II, last of the Hapsburgs, and the French royal family of the Bourbons controlled Spain. In fact, a family pact brought Spain into the French camp as an ally. It is not necessary to go into the many details of Louis XIV's military campaigns; it is important to note that he impoverished France thereby, cost the people many lives, and laid some of the bricks for the French Revolution less than a century later, in 1789. Of course, French culture, the language and the literature, spread throughout Europe and left lasting impressions and influence in other countries.

Sun King

At home, Louis XIV, as he grew older, became more and more vain; he wanted to be known as the "Sun King," so bright was the radiance of his power. He constructed the beautiful and very costly palace of Versailles outside Paris, as a symbol of his power. Also, Louis XIV greatly encouraged the arts. Although French literature was already in a blossoming state prior to his ascendancy, Louis XIV aided enormously in fostering the brilliance of the "Classical Age" in French culture. Corneille, Racine, and Molière in the theater; Pascal in philosophy; Boileau and La Fontaine in poetry; and the several novelists who cultivated the comparatively new form of the novel, proved that the "Sun King" could put his talents and ambition to useful purpose. Therefore, the "Age of Louis XIV," although exhausting France and partly causing later political upheaval, provided the royal patronage, wealth, and audiences which artists required for their endeavors.

THE THEATER OF MOLIÈRE

The French Theater

During the Middle Ages, the theater was held in very low esteem because of its crude and anticlerical basis on many occasions. However, the theater was very popular during the years prior to Molière's appearance as a dramatist; several companies, particularly Italian, performed regularly in Paris. Some prestige even accrued to the theatrical scene; for example, Cardinal Richelieu, the prime minister of Louis XIII and the real ruler of the country, wrote plays and consequently protected the theater. He even built a theater so that his plays could be staged. Despite the growing popularity of the stage and some respect for it, the profession was looked down upon as degrading. In the provinces, the strolling companies suffered from hostile audiences, who refused to pay if they disliked the shows, and uncertain living quarters and provisions.

If any literary fame could be won in the theater, it had to be in the field of tragedy and not comedy. For example, French tragedy is generally considered to date from about 1599 until 1630 with the plays of Hardy and Mairet. The first figure of importance was Pierre Corneille (1606-1684) who set the pattern with *The Cid* (Le Cid) in 1636. Drama must follow the rules of the three unities: time, place, and action; there is no mixture of the tragic and comic; and the subjects are historical. Duty and the will, supreme over love, are the outstanding themes. Later, Jean Racine (1639-1699), in such plays as *Phèdra* (Phèdre) in 1677, followed in Corneille's path but aimed for a high degree of poetry and passion in the drama. Therefore, tragedy dominated the French theater during Molière's lifetime and was looked upon as the highest form of dramatic art. In the "Classical Age" all art must follow the pattern of the classics, the Greek and Roman models, and adhere to the theories of Aristotle.

Original Form

However, the theoreticians of the drama set up no rules for comedy. Scaliger, one of these dogmatists, claimed that only three things were needed: an easy and common style, a complicated plot, and a happy ending. Although Greek and Roman comedy was known, and the Italian and Spanish comedies, and even works of Shakespearean origin, were played, no great attention was devoted to the theatrical form and techniques of the comedy. Molière appeared to fill this void in the theater and also to create a highly original form. In the tragedy, psychological depths and profound **themes** were being exploited by Corneille and the young Racine. Aristocratic audiences, particularly the immediate royal circle, preferred the tragedy; some nobles encouraged the comedy but believed that this aspect of the theater belonged to the common people and the growing middle class.

INFLUENCES ON MOLIÈRE

Literary Backgrounds Of Molière

The first influence or contact with the history of theater is found in Molière's formal education in the Jesuit schools. At least, he must have read certain of the works of Menander, Plautus, and Terence, but these dramatists, although possibly providing some of the technical skills for the later Molière, did not write the lofty and poetic comedy he perfected. Likewise, Molière may have acted in early stage productions of the Jesuits and may have watched actors in shows during free hours. La Grange, an immediate source for much information, but unfortunately not always reliable, suggests these sources of Molière's art.

The Farce

The first clearly defined source of influence on Molière is the native or French tradition of the farce. The farce was usually a short skit, broadly humorous and satirical of society or people, which had as its primary, if not sole, aim to provoke hearty laughter. Medieval in origin, the farce still enjoyed popularity in Paris and the provinces during Molière's day, so that he must have watched it being performed if he watched anything. Molière first won Louis XIV's admiration and that of the theatrical public with farces and he constantly returned to this source; for example, his last play, *The Imaginary Invalid*, is largely farcical. Another indigenous influence could well be that of Rabelais, the sixteenth century author of *Gargantua* and *Pantagruel*. Rabelais, with his advocacy of naturalness, racy humor, and social **satire**, has noticeable affinities with Molière.

Of the foreign models, the influence of the Italian commedia dell'arte is undeniable in the development of Molière's theater. The commedia dell'arte is an improvised dialogue performed by actors who maintain a rigid identification. For example, today one might cite the figure of "Uncle Sam" as a commedia dell'arte character: the patriotic costume, the hat, and the beard compose a form of mask which makes the performer immediately recognizable in his role. At that time, masks were definitely part of the commedia dell'arte. A group of actors would perform a playlet, their roles easily known by the viewers, and they would compose their lines as they went along. Each actor would, of course, have to talk and behave according to his station in life and the part he was interpreting. Historical research has shown that this Italian dramatic form was extremely popular in France, especially in the South close to the Italian borders, and also that the commedia dell'arte had already influenced the old French farce. The Italian background of Molière's theatrical art is clear from his early farces. Also, French tragedy was a somewhat rigid dramatic form, and the actors were not permitted much freedom of action on the stage. Molière emphasizes movement, and his plots express a dynamic quality; for example, seldom is the stage restricted to one single character and rarely do soliloquies rule the scenes. Plot is sacrificed to humor in the commedia dell'arte and tragedy is not employed. These characteristics also define Molière's plays.

Spanish Influence

Of lesser importance than the Italian influence, but important to the study of Molière's theatrical background, is the sure knowledge he had of the Spanish comedia. The Spanish drama, known and admired in France, had already been imitated by Corneille in two of his own productions. Spain, although in decline, still exercised political and consequently cultural and literary influence in Europe and in France. Scholars have attempted to compare and contrast speeches and plot situations with Spanish drama, but no definite appraisal can be made of Spanish influence. It exists in Molière, possibly through Italian translations, and it is evident that he knew the Spanish comedia from its performances in France. However, Molière could have reacted negatively against the Spanish background; he rejects lyrical outbursts and exalted sentiments and prefers to depict the humorous warfare between a character and his environment.

LANGUAGE OF MOLIÈRE

Language

In this same vein, the influence and importance of Molière can be analyzed in his use of the French language and of speech in general. In the first place, Molière is varied in his plays; he utilizes prose and verse at will. His most philosophical play, *The Misanthrope*, is in verse; and his continuing popular hit, *The Would-Be Gentleman*, in prose. In fact, there is a humorous speech in the latter play about the differences between prose and verse. Another of Molière's contributions is having the characters employ the language of their social rank: servants speak in a common vernacular and nobles in a refined, exaggerated style even within the same scene.

Molière unfortunately left few documents about his dramatic theories but he did write in the preface to Tartuffe that "things and not words should be debated . . . most disagreements come about by not understanding and enclosing opposite things in the same word . . . One must remove the veil, of ambiguity." Thus, Molière avoids an indirect and flowery language. One of his favorite whipping boys in the theater was the exaggerated and flowery style then in vogue in the capital. He lends a conversational tone to his characters' speech which is lively and lifelike. If people speak simply, less misunderstanding occurs. For example, Molière uses repetition of words to extract distinct meanings and **connotations** from different forms of emphasis and tone. He also uses "and" a great deal to link phrases for more clarity. Nouns seem to be preferred without any qualifying adjectives.

Nevertheless, the language of Molière is colorful and its brusque, brief nature reflects the dramatica need of keeping the audience's attention and imitating natural speech. Molière can ably make use of language to denote differences in personality as well as social rank. In an age of increasing refinement in the usage of the French language, the growing power of the French Academy in matters of grammar and linguistics, and the stratification of society, Molière dignified common speech and the language of peasants and others who were not in political and social power. He also pointed to the dangers when language is removed from the majority of the public; language must be kept realistic, or the increasing failure to communicate will cause arguments and disorder.

Popular Speech

Certainly Molière is more effective in prose than in verse; his intellectual powers of **irony**, sarcasm, etc., are effective but they lack popular appeal. Molière remains a master at restoring popular speech. In more literary exercises, he follows the dramatic tradition of Corneille and Racine as an imitator but not as a trailblazer. Sainte-Beuve, the nineteenth century French critic, wrote of Molière's style that "to love him sincerely, is to have a guarantee against many a defect and many a fault; it is to be antipathetic to all pedantry, all artificiality of style, all affectation of language."

THE PRECIOUS DAMSELS

THE PLAY

CHARACTERS

La Grange, young gentleman Du Croisy, young gentleman Gorgibus, well-to-do bourgeois or middle-class citizen Magdelon, daughter of Gorgibus Cathos, niece of Gorgibus Marotte, maid in Gorgibus' home Almanzor, servant in Gorgibus' home Mascarille, servant of La Grange Jodelet, servant of Du Croisy Lucille, Célimène, neighbors

SETTING

The house of Gorgibus in Paris.

INTRODUCTION

La Grange and Du Croisy are complaining to each other about the way Magdelon and Cathos are treating them. The two country girls are putting on "precious" airs which are making them ridiculous and which are annoying the two young men a great deal. La Grange explains that "preciosity" is the latest fad in Paris: nothing is said or done directly, everything must be hinted at, and conversation becomes boring because of these snobbish and pedantic ways. La Grange wants to get revenge on the girls and starts to explain his plan to Du Croisy when Gorgibus enters. Gorgibus realizes that the two young gentlemen are very dissatisfied. When they leave, he tells Marotte to have Magdelon and Cathos come down at once.

When the two girls appear, Gorgibus scolds them for not acting politely to the gentlemen whom he wants them to mart. The girls consider Gorgibus too old-fashioned, middle-class, and practical. They want more romance and excitement as in novels. They also want flatteries and attentions paid to them by the suitors. Magdelon and Cathos criticize the young men for being too unrefined since they are not dressed according to the latest Parisian fashions. The father can stand no more when they demand to be called by more aristocratic and classical names than their family names. He tells them bluntly that it is time they were married and gave him some peace of mind. He gives them this choice: get married or enter a convent.

After Gorgibus leaves the room. Magdelon and Cathos try to make Marotte speak in a more "precious" manner, but the maid only makes fun of them. She tells the girls that a marquis has just arrived to see them, and the two girls hurry upstairs to prepare themselves to receive this important visitor. Mascarille, disguised as the nobleman, enters and tries without success to avoid paying the sedan-chair bearers. La Grange has arranged Mascarille's appearance to avenge himself on the two girls. Mascarille has all the mannerisms of the "precious" fad and outdoes Magdelon and Cathos in his exaggerated airs and speech. Each person tries increasingly to outdo the other as the conversation develops. The girls are completely deceived and duped by Mascarille.

Mascarille discusses the advantages of Paris society and emphasizes to the girls his importance in the life of the city. He assures them that he can open all doors for them. Without his help they will never be able to become "precious damsels." Magdelon wants to belong to this world of smartness and elegance. She praises the way of life of gossip, parties, and the social whirl in general. Mascarille promises to establish an academy or club in their home so that they will be the center of the "precious" society. He recites one of his poems for them, which they applaud; the poem is quite meaningless but written in the flowery style then in fashion.

Mascarille sings very badly. Magdelon and Cathos applaud. He offers to take them to the theater since he has offered also to encourage the author by applauding before the play starts. Mascarille deceives Magdelon and Cathos so thoroughly that they end by considering themselves far below his station in life. At this moment, Jodelet, the servant of Du Croisy, enters. He too pretends to be a nobleman, and the two servants act in such "precious" fashion in speech and manners that the girls believe they have been accepted into the most elegant circles of Paris. The servants brag that they have been very brave soldiers in the service of the king and relate bigger and bigger lies about their military campaigns and wounds.

Mascarille and Jodelet decide to have a party, and two neighbors, Lucille and Célimène, join the group. The fiddlers begin to play and dancing is organized. However, La Grange and Du Croisy appear and begin to beat the servants. Their explanation, with apologies to the girls, is that the servants have taken the clothes of their masters in order to amuse themselves. The two gentleman pretend to be very sorry for what has happened to Magdelon and Cathos. La Grange and Du Croisy say they will allow the girls to love their servants but only in their true state. They order the servants stripped of the finery of the gentlemen. The girls are humiliated at the disclosure of La Grange and Du Croisy.

Gorgibus enters and tells the girls how their behavior has disgraced him. They have made themselves ridiculous by their complete acceptance of false standards of social conduct and literary values. With Gorgibus' attack on the entire concept of "preciosity," the play ends on a humorous and moral tone.

Comment

The principal purpose of the play, which accounted for its success and which provided Molière with his first acceptance in Paris, was to attack "preciosity." This literary movement had contributed something of value to French life and culture: manners and speech became more refined, the French language developed in richness and precision, and the individual gentleman and lady expressed themselves more politely. Molière was satirizing the vulgarization and affectations of those who were extremists in the school of "preciosity." His main weapon in the attack was humor, because he saw that the "precious" school had lost sight of reality and become isolated from the facts of life. There are perhaps two reasons for the success of *The Precious Damsels:* those who were not in agreement with the attitudes of "preciosity" saw confirmation of their objections in Molière, and those who favored "preciosity" were able to observe how foolishly they acted at times.

The play is very short, in one act and in prose, and does not have the sharpness, profundity, and personal applications of Molière's later dramas. However, one must bear in mind that the theatrical devices and stock characters are already in evidence in this early play. The play is fresh and spontaneous and marked a new trend in the French theater.

THE PRECIOUS DAMSELS

CHARACTER ANALYSES

MAGDELON AND CATHOS

They symbolize country girls attracted by the superficial sophistication of the big city, Paris. They reject common sense and moderation as rules of behavior and have become overly impressed by the appearances of society. In order to show that they are not naive and uneducated, they accept too wholeheartedly the prevailing fashion of "preciosity." They do not dare to criticize or reject any of the new ideas for fear of not being regarded highly. They make their crucial mistake by becoming so "precious" that they cannot judge people and a situation realistically and correctly. Thus they are made fools of and are humbled at the drama's conclusion.

LA GRANGE AND DU CROISY

The two young suitors represent the opposite qualities of the girls: reason, moderation, and good sense. Therefore they are in direct opposition to the prevailing social and literary tastes of "preciosity." They appear only at the beginning and at the end of the play but they nevertheless control the action. They have organized the trick upon Magdelon and Cathos, and they provide the solution of the problem by their appearance during the party.

MASCARILLE AND JODELET

The servants are the comic foils for the masters, La Grange and Du Croisy. The two suitors have as their purpose the deflation of the "precious" vogue and the winning of the girls' hearts to simpler ways; the servants look upon this **episode** as a chance to make fun of the noble and snobbish airs of a higher social class. They provide the "slapstick" quality in the comedy.

GORGIBUS

His attitude is that of a middle-class father, interested in practical matters, such as a financially sound marriage for the daughters. Practicality is his main rule of conduct in life. He is uninterested in any matter which does not concern his status in society. In this play, he reflects the feelings of Molière about the extreme ideas of "preciosity," as do the two suitors, La Grange and Du Croisy.

THE PRECIOUS DAMSELS

ESSAY QUESTIONS AND ANSWERS

Question: How does Molière ridicule "preciosity" in *The Precious Damsels* (Les Précieuses Ridicules)? What moral does he wish the audience to learn from the play?

Answer: Molière uses characters, dialogue, and plot to criticize and ridicule "preciosity." Magdelon and Cathos, adhering to "precious" ideals, are foolish in themselves, and all the other characters, the suitors, the servants, and the father, by following contrasting paths, emphasize the ridiculousness of the girls' exaggerated airs. The contrasts are so obvious and so overwhelming that the audience can see no merit in the attitude of the girls. Dialogue likewise stresses this use of extremes: the speech of the girls, the gentlemen, and the servants, with the father furnishing the final touch, reflects the great difference between normal, understandable conversation and the affectations and vagueness of the "precious" girls. When the servants, now disguised as noblemen, speak as "preciously" as they can, their ways outdo those of Magdelon and Cathos. Thus there is a double attack on "preciosity" in the dialogue of the play. The plot is simple and direct, unlike the style of "precious" literature, and the audience immediately learns of the scheme being played by Mascarille and Jodelet on behalf of their masters. It is obvious from the start that the girls will be humiliated and humbled. The question is how long it will take them to be taught the needed lesson. The audience wonders only how ridiculous they will make themselves before the true status of the servants is explained to them. From the entrance of the disguised servants, each comic element adds to the coming downfall of "the precious damsels."

Molière wishes to show that men are ridiculous when they do not act naturally. "Preciosity" in its radical fringes lacks good sense, reason, moderation, and practicality. The tendency lacks the quality of viewing life and men with a certain amount of humor. Any attitude that denies these human traits must be deflated, and the adherents of such fashions must see their proud airs and haughty illusions destroyed.

THE SCHOOL FOR WIVES

THE PLAY

CHARACTERS

Arnolphe, or Mr. Delafield Agnes, Arnolphe's ward Horace Alain, Arnolphe's servant Georgette, Alain's wife Chrysalde, Arnolphe's friend Enrique, Chrysalde's brother-in-law Oronte, Horace's father Notary

SETTING

Arnolphe's house and garden

ACT I

Arnolphe and Chrysalde are discussing his plans to marry Agnes. Chrysalde advises against the marriage because Arnolphe's suspicious nature will lead him immediately to suspect his wife of being unfaithful and destroy any hope of a happy marriage. Arnolphe replies that he knows and has heard enough about deceived husbands in the city to be on the alert about Agnes. Chrysalde again counsels Arnolphe that the latter will be observed by all his neighbors for the slightest indication of marital woe, since he has always been ready to laugh at and gossip about such unhappiness in his acquaintances. But Arnolphe is very sure of himself because he is marrying a simple and innocent girl; he prefers to have a stupid wife, obedient and hard-working, than an intelligent and beautiful one. When Agnes was four years old, Arnolphe asked to be her guardian, and her poor mother, delighted at the thought of a protector for a daughter without a dowry, accepted the offer. Agnes has been raised in a convent according to Arnolphe's theory mentioned above, and has been kept isolated from society. Arnolphe invites Chrysalde to dine with the two of them this evening so that the skeptical Chrysalde can observe Agnes' simple-mindedness. For example, Arnolphe laughingly tells his friends, Agnes the other day asked him if children are begotten through the ear.

Chrysalde still doubts Arnolphe's wisdom in the whole affair. For instance, he cannot understand why Arnolphe has taken the name of Mr. Delafield. Arnolphe believes the latter name is more aristocratic and sounds better; he insists that Chrysalde call him by that name instead of his real one. The two friends depart, each thinking that the other is a little crazy for his strange opinions. Arnolphe decides to check up on Agnes and goes upstairs to the isolated living quarters.

Alain and Georgette, the two servants, quarrel about opening the door for their master until he threatens not to feed them other trying to open the door first. The replies of the servants for at least four days. At that point both push and shove each about Agnes during Arnolphe's absence are very unsatisfactory, and his suspicions begin to increase. Agnes enters the room, and

Arnolphe is now satisfied that all is well because she answers as stupidly as ever when he speaks. The fact that she is sewing for him likewise calms his nerves.

Alone, Arnolphe praises himself for having educated such a simpleton for a wife. Horace enters with a letter from his father, Oronte, for Arnolphe. Surprised at the way Horace has grown to manhood over the years, Arnolphe welcomes him and even offers to lend the young man money. Horace eagerly accepts, and Arnolphe is forced to give him money. Horace explains that Oronte is coming soon in person with Enrique, a local man who is returning from America with a fortune.

Arnolphe advises Horace to enjoy the pleasures and women of the city. Horace confides to Arnolphe that he has already started to court a young lady who, although kept alone by a guardian, has responded to his advances. Her guardian, Horace goes on to say, is rather ridiculous and not very intelligent. At the mention of the name "Agnes," Arnolphe is stunned. Horace, thinking he is boring Arnolphe, leaves after saying that he will use the borrowed money to woo Agnes. Arnolphe, known as Mr. Delafield to Horace, the suitor of Agnes, plans to lead Horace on in order to find out everything about the love affair.

ACT II

Arnolphe, having lost Horace's trail in his attempt to discover how successful he has been with Agnes, determines to continue his snoopings. He starts to criticize Alain and Georgette for their carelessness in allowing Horace to see Agnes; then he accuses them of betraying his interests deliberately. It is evident that he is quite upset and does not know which way to turn in this situation. He decides to talk directly with Agnes and endeavor to solve the mystery. Alain and Georgette, alone, discuss his jealousy problem.

Arnolphe returns to the room and prepares for the interview with Agnes. He plans to be astute in the probings of her heart. Arnolphe warns Agnes of the evil effect of gossip and relates what he claims neighbors have reported about a strange man in the house during his absence. Agnes, the product of Arnolphe's education, answers simply and innocently that a man spent a long time in the house. Her story is naive to the point of stupidity: she kept returning bows from a balcony to a young man until nightfall came in order not to seem impolite. The next day, an old woman came to visit her and played on her simplicity and pity by requesting her aid to cure a man wounded by her love. Agnes was told that only the sight of her eyes could cure him and therefore she consented to his visits as often as he wished. Arnolphe, in anguish at each **episode** of the story, begins to realize that part of the fault for Agnes' sweet innocence is his. He sees that his method of education for Agnes has made her an easy victim for Horace or for any young man in general.

There are double meanings in many of the lines between Agnes and Arnolphe. These remarks prove her exceptional simplicity to him and also increase his worry and frustration. Her guardian warns Agnes that her actions are sinful, but she is unconvinced and delights in her growing love for Horace. She wants to get married right away, and Arnolphe announces happily that the marriage can take place that very evening. She is delighted at the prospect of marrying Horace until Arnolphe explains that it will be to someone else. He then forbids her to see Horace any more. She rebels for the first time but Arnolphe is forceful in his orders that she return to her isolated apartment.

ACT III

Arnolphe praises Agnes for having followed his orders: it seems that she threw a brick at Horace the next time he appeared to court her. He then admonishes her about the sinful ways of young men and his own protective role in her life. Finally he decides to talk seriously and privately with Agnes about marriage and the facts of life. Arnolphe has the two servants leave in order to bring the notary for the signing of the marriage contract. In a very long speech, Arnolphe seeks to persuade Agnes of his own merits. He recalls to her that she was penniless without his help and is now being offered the chance to marry into an upper social class, the bourgeoisie or middle class, and that he has determined to marry even after so many years of bachelorhood. She is given admonitions about the married life: obedience, humility, respect, and fidelity will be her watchwords. If she fails in these qualities, then her soul will burn in hell for all eternity. To illustrate better his advice, Arnolphe has Agnes read a set of rules from a marriage booklet. The maxims are written in a very sarcastic tone with a meaning other than that which Arnolphe intended. In general, they comment on the straight and narrow path which women must follow and the freedoms men have.

After Agnes departs with the book of rules, Arnolphe rationalizes his present predicament: he is still better off with the naive and simple Agnes, whom he can mold to his own will, than with an intelligent and shrewd woman who would trick him easily. When Horace enters, Arnolphe is elated and brags to the young man about his own peace of mind as opposed to the youth's defeats in his amorous adventures. Horace sorrowfully narrates how the servants, Alain and Georgette, refuse to allow him inside the house, and how Agnes has thrown a brick at him. In mock sympathy, Arnolphe encourages Horace in his story until he learns that Agnes threw a letter along with the brick. The tables are turned as Arnolphe painfully listens to the love letter of his ward. He regrets that she learned how to write against his orders. It is obvious from the contents of the letter that Agnes is in love with Horace and that she no longer accepts Arnolphe's words of advice. According to Horace, love has won the day, and he promises to punish the villain who has mistreated the girl for so long. Arnolphe tries to leave. In a soliloquy, he bemoans his dilemma: he still loves the girl, and yet he now desires revenge. He finally decides to demonstrate a stoic and brave attitude as he faces her.

ACT IV

Arnolphe has found no trace of sorrow or shame in Agnes. He therefore selects the path of revenge for her deceit and ingratitude. When the notary arrives, Arnolphe assumes an uninterested air and postpones the signing of the marriage contract. The notary leaves with the impression that Arnolphe is a madman. The old man's jealous and suspicious nature continues to get the best of him. He pays the two servants to be more watchful against any effort of Horace to enter the house. He also decides to bribe a cobbler down the street to be a spy, and plans to restrict anyone from entering the house. In short, he wants to prevent any message from Horace reaching Agnes.

Horace comes to confide in Arnolphe his latest adventures with Agnes. He succeeded in seeing her on the balcony, and she invited him to her room. However, her guardian came in and he had to hide in a closet. The anger of Agnes' master is described vividly by Horace, who suspects that his enemy must be aware of the situation. When Horace reveals that he has a date with Agnes for tonight and speaks of the precautions the two of them have taken, Arnolphe is jubilant about the possibility of trapping the lovers. He ponders the irony of fate; he has schemed for years to prevent exactly what is being plotted against him. Chrysalde interrupts to accept the dinner invitation which Arnolphe extended to him earlier in the play. Arnolphe receives Chrysalde rudely and refuses to discuss his marriage plans, which he formerly was eager to do. Chrysalde chides Arnolphe for the undue emphasis he gives to the problem of a deceived husband. Arnolphe has engaged in cruelty, greed, and double-dealing to save his "honor." Chrysalde advises the avoidance of extremes: it is not necessary to adopt the hypocritical standards of some social groups who flaunt this personal tragedy before others, nor is it necessary to adopt the point of view of Arnolphe. Chrysalde advises in short that Arnolphe make the best of it. Marriage is a game of chance; if one loses, one should wait prudently for his luck to change. There could be worse things than an unfaithful wife; a nagging wife is far worse, according to the wise Chrysalde.

After the departure of Chrysalde, whose final piece of wisdom is that Arnolphe do nothing at all about his offended honor, Arnolphe vengefully enlists the support of Alain and Georgette to attack Horace that night. They will hide near the window, and as he reaches the top rung of the ladder, everyone will begin to beat him with sticks. Arnolphe cautions them against uttering his name during the attack. He promises a good reward to Georgette and Alain if all goes well. He welcomes the coming assault as a needed lesson for many lovers of wives in the city.

ACT V

Arnolphe berates the servants for their supposed violent clubbing of Horace. He wanted the boy beaten, but not fatally; blows should have been aimed for his back, not his head. He fears the reaction of Oronte, Horace's father. However, Horace joins Arnolphe and solves the puzzle; he fell from the ladder and pretended to be dead when the attackers examined him. After they left, Agnes came out of the house, and the two of them fled together. Horace again comments on the **irony** of fate for Agnes' guardian, whose latest plot has backfired and brought the lovers closer together. Horace proclaims his true love for Agnes. He does not wish to take advantage of her trust in him; therefore he asks Arnolphe, as his friend, to shelter the girl in his house. Of course, Arnolphe agrees all too willingly to get Agnes back into his hands.

At the garden entrance, Horace hands Agnes over to Arnolphe, who conceals his true identity in a large cloak. When Horace has gone, Arnolphe throws aside the cloak and heaps scorn upon the surprised and terrified Agnes. Agnes defends her conduct on the grounds that she loves Horace and wants to marry him. She rejects any offer of marriage from Arnolphe; she cannot love him and she also refuses to accept the excuse of necessary gratitude as the reason for marriage. Arnolphe is also chided by Agnes for the restricted education he has provided her. At last, Arnolphe appeals to her pity and his love for her. He moans the fate of a man in love with a woman who does not appreciate his affection. When he understands that all the pleas are in vain, he promises to send her to a convent for her misconduct. Alain is ordered to lock her in her room until Arnolphe comes back. As he is about to leave, Horace rushes in, very upset. Oronte, his father, and Enrique, the rich settler from America, are coming to see Arnolphe for the purpose of arranging Horace's marriage. The young man has also found out that the girl selected for his bride is Enrique's daughter. He begs Arnolphe to help him and prevent the marriage to this supposedly unknown girl. Arnolphe mockingly agrees to aid him and again hopes to trap his rival. They discuss their strategy in a corner of the room.

Enrique greets Chrysalde, his brother-in-law, and expresses sorrow that his wife, Chrysalde's sister, died overseas and cannot be here to see this happy day. Enrique insists that Chrysalde approve the choice of Horace for the bridegroom. Arnolphe leaves Horace for a moment to join the new group and to encourage the plans of Enrique for the speedy wedding of Horace. Horace overhears the betrayal of Arnolphe; the latter believes that the young man should have no choice but obedience in the matter. Chrysalde is puzzled at Arnolphe's enthusiasm for the match because the old man does not know the name of the bride. When Arnolphe is called "Mr Delafield," Horace finally realizes who his enemy is. He is in despair until Agnes enters. Then Oronte and Chrysalde solve the mystery: Agnes is the long lost daughter of Enrique, born of a secret marriage. The girl was brought up in the country until her father could return from America a rich man. Now the wedding between Horace and Agnes has been arranged by Enrique and Oronte. Chrysalde moralizes to Arnolphe that since he was so afraid of being deceived in marriage, the best solution is not to marry. Providence takes care of matters, concludes Chrysalde, as Arnolphe leaves in sorrow.

Comment

One must bear in mind the undeniable biographical background of this particular play, which is completely in verse. The role of Arnolphe was played by Molière, and that of Agnes, by Armande Béjart, his bride of about a year. The situation of Arnolphe parallels that of Molière in several aspects. Molière writes and speaks from his own sad experiences when he warns against trying to mold a wife from childhood according to his own standards. He saw the failure of his efforts in Armande whom he had known since her childhood. The marital difficulties he was perhaps already facing were due also to the great age difference between them, similar to that between Arnolphe and Agnes.

In brief, Molière seemed unable to control, according to his own wishes, the inclinations of a young and headstrong wife.

This play is the first comedy in five acts in verse by Molière. Thus he adhered now to the prevailing French classical tradition. He also sought to follow the rule of the three unities: time, place, and action. The story takes place in one day, no matter how illogical it may seem on occasions to have all the action occur within twenty-four hours, and the setting remains the same by using one house, the adjacent garden, and the street as a unit. The action revolves about the efforts of Arnolphe to marry Agnes and so the plot is unified. However, Molière still clung to Roman, Greek, and Italian models in his employment of humor and artificial situations, as in the solution of the mystery of Agnes. Although violence is banished from the stage according to classical rule, which Molière accepts by not showing the scene when Horace is attacked by the servants, there are the farcical encounters with the servants. Molière appeals to the intellectual tastes of the audience by probing Arnolphe's mind in soliloquies. In the various contrasting arguments, as between Arnolphe and Chrysalde, Molière skillfully expounds each point of view.

Nevertheless, the play has been criticized for this static quality; there is basically little action despite the comings and goings of all the characters. Everything is told to the audience instead of the events unfolding in front of the viewers. In fact, the plot is oversimplified and overextended when the length of the play is kept in mind. There are fragmentary elements, as in the scene with the notary which has little to do with the development of the intrigue. The play achieved an immediate success and created such great controversy that in 1663 Molière wrote a reply, *The Critique of The School for Wives*, in which he defended and explained his comedy technique. Molière understood the effect that his new type of comic hit was having with audiences. His use of traditional and foreign sources together with those of French classic art provided the theater with a new direction.

THE SCHOOL FOR WIVES

CHARACTER ANALYSES

Arnolphe

In the portrayal of Arnolphe, Molière approaches the concept of a comedy of character. There are two main aspects to this character: he is of course a comic figure whose plots fail and whose courting of Agnes is ridiculous because of his self-centered nature. His jealous and suspicious ways make him laughable as he loses touch with reality more and more while pursuing his goal of marrying Agnes. At the same time, there is another dimension to Arnolphe: he is a tragic figure, the man of forty-two who wishes to marry the girl of eighteen. He cannot grasp the girl's unwillingness to marry him. Should not gratitude, desire for a higher station in life, and his own outstanding qualities (which really are defects) be reason enough? Arnolphe does not understand that love is the first requisite of marriage for Agnes and that youth seeks youth as a partner in life.

Agnes

Agnes symbolizes the predicament of the young girl who has been subjected to a strict and narrow education without any rights to her own future. She expresses the desire of women to be emancipated and to select their own husbands on the basis of their own love. Youth must be served and cannot blindly obey the dictates of parents and elders. Emotion, feeling, and sentiment must occupy a more important place than future security and social standing. In her innocence and simplicity, Agnes speaks the truth and sees matters more clearly than the double-dealing Arnolphe.

Horace

Like Agnes, Horace symbolizes youth at the mercy of the plans of parents and elders. In his youth, he is honest and forthright to the point of trusting Arnolphe completely without any thought of deceit on the latter's part. Horace is enthusiastic and resourceful; he plans only to win the lady of his heart and tries all ways to see her. Since the two of them complement each other so well, the sympathies of Molière are with them, and their marriage should take place.

Chrysalde, Enrique, And Oronte

The three middle-class citizens, particularly Chrysalde, are men of the world who accept life as it is. They rationalize about the problems of children, good marriages, youth, etc. In Arnolphe, they see extremity which cannot be accepted by their bourgeois standards. As a result, they are the ones who are pleased and satisfied by the turn of events at the play's end. Good sense and moderation have triumphed again.

Alain And Georgette

As usual, the servants provide a broad comic appeal or slapstick quality in the drama. In their stupidity and crudity, they complement on a lower plane the idealistic virtues of the lovers, Horace and Agnes. Although fearful of Arnolphe and greedy for his money, they laugh at his foolish ways just as their superiors, the middle-class characters, do.

THE SCHOOL FOR WIVES

ESSAY QUESTIONS AND ANSWERS

Question: What does Molière intend by the title of his play, *The School for Wives* (*L'École Des Femmes*)?

Answer: Molière is a moralist: he wishes the audience to leave the theater with a practical lesson which they will employ in their everyday lives. He is seeking to explain his theories about the education of women. He does not approve of the early training of Agnes in the convent which made her ignorant of the basic facts of life and completely submissive to her guardian. When Agnes comes into contact with the realities of life, that is to say, her meetings with Horace, she begins to develop naturally. Molière is seeking to strike a balance between the overly educated "precious" woman portrayed in *The Precious Damsels* and the uneducated Agnes. Molière advocates freedom and emancipation for women but he does not want them to give up the traditional virtues of love for a husband, interest in his welfare, and care for the home. Happiness will come to Agnes and Horace because Agnes accepts these standards. In other words, Molière chooses the middle path in the education of women-for their own peace of mind and for that of their husbands-to-be.

Question: What is the role of chance and fate in the comedy?

Answer: Arnolphe pits himself and his intelligence against chance and fate at the very beginning of the play when he defies the warnings of Chrysalde about being deceived. Despite the fact that Arnolphe has all the advantages in the struggle against Horace for Agnes, such as being the confidant of the young man and thus knowing his strategy, he is outmaneuvered every time by chance operating through coincidences. He constantly encounters Horace when he thought he had vanquished his rival. Little by little, fate and chance wear down Arnolphe's confidence and his pride until he starts to talk of the stars working against him. He is humbled and humiliated by chance and fate when he appeals to Agnes to marry him out of pity for his love and gratitude for the upbringing he has given her. At the end of the play, he is so thoroughly beaten by destiny and ill-luck in the appearance of Enrique and Oronte that he slinks away without a word. Man must use his reason and good judgment but he must not forget about the unknown factors in life which may decide the victory for him. For Molière, life still contains mysteries which are beyond the grasp of man's intelligence.

TARTUFFE

THE PLAY

CHARACTERS

Mrs. Pernelle, Orgon's mother Orgon Elmire, Orgon's wife Damis, Orgon's son, Elmire's stepson Mariane, Orgon's daughter, stepdaughter of Elmire Valère Cléante, Orgon's brother-in-law, Elmire's brother Tartuffe Dorine, Mariane's friend Mr. Loyal, bailiff Policeman Flipote, Mrs. Pernelle's servant

SETTING

The home of Orgon in Paris.

ACT I

A family quarrel is in progress with Mrs. Pernelle who is very dissatisfied with the way her son's household is being managed. She criticizes the children for their manners and especially rebukes Elmire for her extravagance. Elmire is not setting a good example as a stepmother, and Mrs. Pernelle scolds the entire family for their disregard of Tartuffe. Everyone objects to his presence in the house, his inquisitiveness and his tyranny, except Mrs. Pernelle. Damis is the most outspoken and calls Tartuffe a pious fraud. They call him a hypocrite and insist that he is enriching himself at their expense. They also mistrust his servant, Laurent. Mrs. Pernelle replies to these charges with the admonition to follow the virtuous path of Tartuffe. Tartuffe hates sin and is only trying to save their souls from eternal damnation. Dorine cannot accept Tartuffe's order that they not be allowed visitors and accuses him of being emotionally interested in Elmire. Mrs. Pernelle is unmoved by these accusations and praises Tartuffe's command not to have visits since visitors only cause scandal. Cléante attempts to answer her by advocating that they live innocently and let the neighbors talk. Nothing can stop gossip anyway, once gossipers decide to slander someone. Dorine says that the neighbors talk about other people to conceal their own misdeeds. Mrs. Pernelle counterattacks by citing Orante, a neighbor, as an example of a virtuous and religious woman, but Dorine recalls Orante's age and her previous wild life. When society forgot her, she forgot society, but not before. Envy, not charity, is the present explanation of Orante's hypocritical behavior.

Mrs. Pernelle, who has been answered on each of her defenses by members of the family and who senses that she cannot persuade them to change their minds and accept Tartuffe, utters a long final speech before her departure. Her son did right in admitting Tartuffe to the house and encouraging him to reform this house of evil. She warns them that unless they give up parties and dances and follow the straight and narrow path, she will not visit them again. Cléante and Dorine remain after the others accompany Mrs. Pernelle to the door. They debate the reasons for the overwhelming influence Tartuffe has over Orgon. Orgon, prior to Tartuffe's arrival, was a man of good sense and judgment. Now Orgon has conceded to Tartuffe the complete direction of his household, treats him as a bosom friend, only sees virtue in him, and gives him money. The other women return, glad to be rid of Mrs. Pernelle. Damis asks Cléante to intercede with Orgon about Mariane's marriage to Valère, which Tartuffe is vigorously opposing.

Orgon comes in after the others leave except for Cléante, who feels obliged to greet his brother-in-law, and Dorine. Orgon shows no interest in his wife's illness the previous night and is concerned only about Tartuffe's welfare. To each explanation of Dorine, he replies. "And Tartuffe?" Dorine leaves the room in anger, and Cléante tries to make Orgon see the foolishness of his conduct. He warns Orgon about the spell which Tartuffe seems to have cast over him. Orgon counsels Cléante to come under that same magic in which all worldly worries vanish and peace of mind is gained. He even goes so far as to say that the death of members of his own family would not bother him. Then Orgon explains how he made the acquaintance of Tartuffe: he noticed the pious devotion of Tartuffe at church, his fervent kissing of the church floor, and his generosity in always running ahead of Orgon to give him holy water. After he brought Tartuffe home with him, everything began to prosper, and he now has a loyal and attentive friend who tries to improve conditions even more. Cléante thinks Orgon is crazy, and Orgon accuses Cléante of being irreligious and in danger of being denounced to the authorities.

Cléante can bear no more. He states forcefully that true religion does not signify the blind acceptance of performances and appearances. He emphasizes the difference between piety and hypocrisy. Why will not man stay within the bounds of reason and pursue the middle path? Why will not man distinguish between appearance and reality? He aims his main attack at religious hypocrisy; he bitterly denounces those who use religion for their own ends and destroy their opponents by their false piety. He praises those who practice as well as preach religion; he advocates the aim of living a good life, hating the sin but not the sinner. Insulted by this diatribe against Tartuffe, Orgon wants to leave, but Cléante asks about the marriage plans of Valère and Mariane. Orgon answers briefly and rudely that he "will follow the will of heaven" and Cléante knows that trouble is ahead.

ACT II

Orgon and Mariane talk about her wedding, and he stresses the need for her obedience to his wishes. She agrees until he announces that he intends Tartuffe to be her husband. She refuses to marry him, and the two begin to quarrel. Noticing Dorine who entered unnoticed, Orgon scolds her for being an eavesdropper. She defends herself by trying to show how foolish he is in his admiration and defense of Tartuffe. For example, she does not understand why he wants Tartuffe for a son-in-law since he is penniless. When Orgon justifies his decision by stating that Tartuffe has sacrificed earthly goods for eternal rewards by not claiming property rightfully his which would make him a landed squire, Dorine claims that these boasts are not signs of a devout humility.

Dorine appeals to Orgon's love for his daughter and her future happiness. Mariane will be wretched with such a husband as Tartuffe, and this causes infidelity in wives. Therefore Orgon will be responsible for any mistakes she may make. Orgon objects to Valère because he has heard the young man is a freethinker, plays cards, and does not attend church regularly. Dorine states that love will be lacking in this marriage and the match can only terminate in tragedy, but Orgon believes that the piety of Tartuffe will bind the two together in happy union. He finally threatens to strike Dorine unless she remains silent and this show of temper is hardly indicative of a pious humility to Dorine. Dorine keeps making snide comments as Orgon praises the qualities of Tartuffe to Mariane. Whenever he turns to slap her, she keeps quiet. Dorine at last flees from Orgon's rage as he fails to convince Mariane that obedience and respect are due him in this matter of the proposed marriage to Tartuffe. Orgon is so angry he cannot continue the conversation and goes into the garden. Then Dorine returns to encourage Mariane in her rebellion. Dorine feels that if Tartuffe is so pleasing to Orgon and not to Mariane, then Tartuffe should be married to Orgon and not to her. Mariane loves only Valère and threatens to kill herself to escape marriage to Tartuffe. Dorine mockingly replies that this is a marvelous remedy for not solving a problem.

TARTUFFE

CHARACTER ANALYSES

TARTUFFE

Although the entrance of Tartuffe is delayed until the third act, the audience has been introduced to him through the speeches of all the other characters in the first two acts. Thus Tartuffe is already revealed as a hypocrite who uses religion and pious talk to win power and money. When he finally appears, his words and actions confirm the impressions conveyed previously. So thoroughly has this groundwork been built up that Tartuffe never does indicate to the audience his true and innermost feelings in any asides, soliloquies, or even a farewell speech as he is being led away in Act V. Tartuffe is essentially a cautious and suspicious individual with a keen intuitive sense who plans and calculates his moves. Thus he does not speak too often for fear of betraying himself. His sole weakness is the passion for Orgon's wife, Elmire. In the love scenes, he comes closest to indicating some aspects of his secret thoughts and aspirations. He is the symbol of religious hypocrisy.

ORGON

While Tartuffe stands for religious hypocrisy, the role of Orgon is considerably more complex to analyze. On the stage Molière played the part of Orgon, which may indicate that he attached more importance to that character than to Tartuffe. In the first place, Orgon is very obviously the dupe of Tartuffe; he has accepted everything the latter has told him and is his complete victim. He refuses to believe what his own wife and children, as well as his friends, repeat about the dangerous course he is traveling. So radically does he show himself duped that he declares that the deaths of his own family would mean nothing now that he has enjoyed the spiritual wisdom of Tartuffe. This attitude is, of course, in complete and total contradiction to any valid religious feeling. Orgon is even prepared to sacrifice his material comforts and those of his family by disinheriting his son and making Tartuffe his heir.

On another level, Orgon shows serious defects of character which have nothing to do with the evil influence of Tartuffe. He is vain and domineering; his wife and children affirm their love and obedience but he wants absolute power over them. He wishes the relationship to be that of master and slave. He is an extremist: under Tartuffe's control, he ingenuously sets out to be sweet and angelic to other men; when he realizes the wicked aspect of Tartuffe's domination, he determines to be the opposite, diabolical in his dealings with other men. He cannot engage in a dialogue with his fellows; he insists upon imposing his will upon all those around him. In certain measure, he is responsible for Tartuffe's success; he hopes that through Tartuffe, he can restore his supremacy over the household. Consequently he symbolizes the increasing power which the middle-class parent exercised over the members of the family and their futures, and the lack of freedom and choice for the children.

CLÉANTE

Cléante is the man of the world, the individual who remains outside of society and can therefore look at the course of events calmly and rationally. The counterpart of Tartuffe, he is the man of moderation, patience, and reasonableness, who never adopts an extremist attitude. In his dialogues with Tartuffe, he praises piety which is not boastful and ostentatious. He defends religious virtues when qualified by common sense. He counsels Orgon not to believe Tartuffe because he is a radical, and yet, he refuses to approve of violence when the family wants to beat Tartuffe up. He is the man who believes in law as the recourse for justice and order. His prevailing mood is also that of a mild skepticism; he accepts nothing in its entirety without analyzing the implications, and he rejects nothing until he has studied all the aspects. Cléante is the model of the solid citizen of his day.

DORINE

Dorine represents naturalness. She is blunt and biting in all her reactions. She does not have to study in detail all the ramifications of a problem; she speaks her mind and always advocates action. She reconciles Valère and Mariane after their quarrel, spurs them on in the activity against Orgon's schemes, and harasses Orgon to the point of distraction with her sarcastic comments. Although a minor character, she plays an important part in Tartuffe's and Orgon's downfall by her encouragement of their opponents.

VALÈRE, MARIANE, AND DAMIS

The first two are the young lovers so common in Molière's plays who have to battle parental opposition and tyranny. Damis is the son who lives in fear that he will be disinherited by a father for lack of obedience. He is youth clamoring to be heard and in rebellion against family domination. He is also headstrong and lacks common sense and worldly experience in his problems.

ELMIRE AND MRS. PERNELLE

These two figures form contrasts which are somewhat striking: Elmire is the long-suffering and faithful wife who exists at the mercy of her husband, has very little to say in household decisions, and in addition encounters the problems of a second wife and stepmother. For instance, she must undergo the insults and complaints of Orgon's mother, Mrs. Pernelle, without showing any sign of bad temper. Mrs. Pernelle is the prototype of her son and considers Tartuffe to be just the person to set the family on the right path. There is an ironic touch in her refusal to believe her son's denunciation of Tartuffe, since this was exactly his reaction when Elmire and the others criticized Tartuffe.

TARTUFFE

ESSAY QUESTIONS AND ANSWERS

Question: What is the attitude of religion on the part of Molière in Tartuffe?

Answer: Molière is no fanatic in favor of religion or against religion. He is amazingly tolerant in France of the seventeenth century which witnessed bitter and violent quarrels on the question of religion. Cléante would seem to fit best the description of Molière's attitude. In all matters of religion, a healthy skepticism should be the order of the day. All hypocrisy and affectation, all criticism and meddling regarding one's neighbors, any attempts at conversion, and certainly any persecution of opposing beliefs should be abolished. Religion is an intimate and personal affair for man; it should be observed simply and privately. It likewise may be said that Molière lets religion alone, and he wants religion to let him alone. While he seems to have practiced the rudiments of a religion, he never interested himself unduly in rites and ceremonies.

Molière cannot advocate any exalted or mystic side of religion. Common sense, reason, and moderation in addition to a skeptical viewpoint are the best criteria for man. He believes in the improvement of humanity, if it is possible, by human virtues and is not motivated by any afterthought of eternity or immortality. Religion consequently should be practical; it should seek to raise the level of human behavior. Molière demonstrates in Tartuffe the evil and harm which can befall humanity by the perversion of spiritual values.

Question: How does Molière use **satire** and humor in Tartuffe?

Answer: Because of the explosive topic he was dealing with in Tartuffe, Molière refrained from the slapstick common in other comedies. The comic element is principally derived from the fact that the characters, particularly Tartuffe and Orgon, make themselves ridiculous and do not realize it. There are always two meanings in the dialogue: the one the characters understand, and the true meaning which the audience grasps. The more importance the two main characters give themselves and the more they express their will, the more the audience laughs at their false and illogical conduct. Thus the humor of Tartuffe derives not from contrived situations and mistaken identities but from a more intellectual base. Language and attitude lift Tartuffe and Orgon to the heights of foolishness. Of course, the humorous approach of Dorine must be less refined because she is of a different social class.

Once the humorous aspect of ridiculous postures and attitudes is understood, and the audience has to laugh at these foibles, the more profound quality, that of **satire**, can be unfolded. At this point, the audience can hardly fail to accept the victims of Molière's **satire**. How can one defend such a humorous and ridiculous person, idea, or belief? First one laughs and later one comes to comprehend the purpose for which Molière is making one laugh. The **satire** on society, fanaticism, extremism, and tyranny is never heavy-handed with Molière; it is always veiled in logical argument and the calmness of reason.

Question: Discuss the intervention of the king in Tartuffe.

Answer: Dramatically weak but psychologically sound in preventing adverse criticism, the insertion of Louis XIV into the play follows the common portrayal of the monarch during the seventeenth century. European kings were asserting their "divine right" to rule, and Louis XIV, in his desire for an absolute monarchy, demanded flattery and complete obedience from his subjects. Molière conveys the impression that the king, if he knows of crime and evil within the nation, will remedy the situation. There are some rather interesting aspects to this problem. Obviously the monarch in such an exalted position cannot be aware of all the happenings within his realm; this may represent a snide commentary on power placed in one individual. When anything amiss within the country is brought to the king's attention, he corrects the error. All the characters of the play practically fall on their hands and knees at the end in admiration of their sovereign. It has been suggested that Molière is really attacking the monarchy for exalting itself so above the people; that is to say, one idol, established religion in the form of Tartuffe, has been replaced by another, the established monarchy.

Therefore, the intervention of the king may serve as a form of social criticism for Molière by causing people to laugh or at least smile at their own incredible acceptance of authority. However, this assumption must yield to the first consideration that Molière had to curry royal favor for protection. He is indeed making a theatrical commentary on the position of Louis XIV and the attitude of the French about their form of government. The role of the king, in any case, is quite unique in the theater of Molière: he never again attempted to portray Louis XIV in any drama.

Question: How is the **theme** of perception developed in the play?

Answer: Perception is one of the dominant ideas of Tartuffe, especially in the interpretation of the principal character. Tartuffe is never, within the drama, caught in a lie; he even confesses the truth to Orgon in the confrontation scene after the **episode** with his wife. The audience has been well aware of Tartuffe's many faults before he appears on the stage; the puzzlement will come from the delay in unmasking the villain. The great surprise is Orgon's failure at discernment, particularly after the exposure of Tartuffe. Another surprise is the lack of perception in Orgon's mother when the son finally realizes Tartuffe's guilt.

This lack of discernment denotes that Orgon and his mother had no true idea of spiritual values and the worth of a person beyond the surface appearance. In other words, they are lacking in true moral virtues and are themselves exactly what Tartuffe is-hypocrites. Only the king shows lucid perception when he sees through Tartuffe; the latter has not told any falsehoods and on the contrary has presented Louis XIV with clear and sufficient evidence of the truth. Molière has emphasized the lack of perception in Orgon and the mother in order to show the dangers of failing in discernment.

THE MISANTHROPE

THE PLAY

CHARACTERS

Alceste) Philinte) Oronte) Gentlemen of the Court Acaste) Clitandre)

Célimène) Éliante, Célimène's cousin) Ladies of the Court Arsinoé)

Basque, Célimène's footman Officer of the Court Du Bois, Alceste's servant

SETTING

The home of Célimène in Paris.

ACT I

Philinte and Alceste are quarreling over the former's flattering conduct with someone whom Alceste now realizes that Philinte hardly knows. Alceste says that a man should be sincere and only speak the truth; he criticizes the elaborate etiquette of the Court in which there is no distinction made between friend and acquaintance, ally and enemy. He advocates complete frankness whereas Philinte responds that one cannot always converse the way one feels. It is necessary to be tactful with both friend and foe. Alceste has witnessed so much hypocrisy that he hates all mankind. He hates the wicked for their misconduct and also those who do nothing to prevent evil. He is tempted to flee to a desert and become a hermit. Philinte counsels him that nothing he can do will change mankind in general and that people are beginning to notice his ridiculous behavior. According to Philinte, the virtuous man should be prudent and tolerant; otherwise, he will become the source of evil by his radical manners. He admits the need of reforms but accepts life calmly and philosophically.

Alceste is involved in a lawsuit and insists that he is right or he is wrong. He refuses to take any measures to prevent his opponent from using dishonest measures. He would rather lose the case than prepare for it in any other way than on the facts themselves. Philinte then brings up the matter of the lady whom Alceste loves. Philinte cannot understand why Alceste has chosen Célimène who represents all the faults about which Alceste is so bitter. Why has he not selected Éliante and Arsione who seem to follow his philosophy? Alceste is well aware of Célimène's faults and failings but is so charmed by her that he believes he can reform her after marriage. Philinte is not so sure that Célimène loves Alceste; he prefers her cousin, Éliante, as a more suitable wife for his friend. Alceste confesses that his reason tells him so at times, but the power of love outweighs reason.

Oronte, another influential gentleman of the Court, enters and flatters Alceste that he agrees with him and wants to be his friend and ally. Alceste, adhering to his code of strict sincerity and bluntness in speech, declines to unite with Oronte at once on the grounds that they should see first if their characters are compatible. Friendship should be formed slowly and by steps to make sure it is lasting. Oronte, much impressed by Alceste's frankness, promises his help with the king should Alceste ever find himself in trouble. At the same time, he shows Alceste a **sonnet** he has written and asks an opinion about it. Alceste states that his reaction will be honest and direct and Oronte insists that this is the report he wishes. During the reading by Oronte, Philinte makes innocent, vague, and complimentary remarks about the poem, and Alceste, criticizing his friend for such lies, shows his displeasure at the verses. Alceste begins his criticism with the warning that an author should not hasten to publish his thoughts. He tries to soften the coming blow by quoting an **episode** with another acquaintance in which he told the man to avoid temptation from now on and not discuss his writings. When Oronte keeps demanding the critical analysis of the poem, Alceste then denounces the poetry as affected and meaningless. True poetry must be natural; it must reflect the emotions and appeal to the heart of man, according to Alceste.

Oronte is highly insulted and defends his poem as excellent. He challenges Alceste to write one like it, and Alceste admits he could compose one just as bad. Philinte at last has to intervene to prevent a quarrel from breaking out. Oronte departs as an enemy, and Philinte tries to warn Alceste about the dangers he is creating for himself because of this tactless attitude. Alceste then flies into a rage against Philinte and wants to be left completely alone. Philinte proves himself a true friend by refusing to leave Alceste alone in this increasingly difficult situation.

ACT II

Alceste is scolding Célimène about her flirtatious manner toward every man who approaches her. She denies any overtures and gestures on her part and blames all the attention she gets on her charming and attractive personality. He is particularly angered by her reaction to Clitandre who he finds lacking in any virtues and one of the most notorious members of the Court. Célimène explains that she wishes his help in winning a lawsuit; Alceste prefers that she lose the case rather than compromise herself with Clitandre. Clitandre is evidently under the suspicion of Alceste, and he shows himself increasingly jealous. Although each states love for the other, both have complaints against one another. Acaste is announced, and another quarrel breaks out. Alceste complains that he can never be alone with Célimène and that she is constantly receiving these visitors who are the parasites of the Court. She explains that while all these individuals may not be able to help her, they can harm her if she is not attentive to them. At the announcement that Clitandre is coming in also, Alceste withdraws in anger despite the pleas of Célimène to remain.

However, when Clitandre and Acaste enter, Alceste reappears in order to make Célimène choose between them and him. Célimène ignores him and engages in the exact type of gossip and hypocritical dialogue which Alceste detests. Alceste at last begins to quarrel with Clitandre who cleverly replies that the fault is Célimène's since they are at her home. To the surprise of Alceste, Célimène joins in the comments of Clitandre and the others against him. He argues that true love should have no room for flattery but only for the truth. The others respond that defects become virtues in the eyes of lovers and so the truth is not objective. Alceste, realizing that he stands alone in his opinions and that the group is united in opposition to him, refuses to leave the house until the others depart. At this critical moment, an officer enters with the order that Alceste is to appear at the Court. Philinte believes that the dispute with Oronte is the cause of this summons; Alceste stubbornly insists that he will not deny or retract his opinion of the poem. However, he departs hastily for the Court as the group and Célimène laugh heartily at his nervousness.

ACT III

Clitandre and Acaste discuss their mutual love for Célimène. Acaste has to admit that she has given him no signs of responding favorably to his feelings. The two rivals then come to a gentlemen's agreement: if Célimène gives any clear indication that she prefers one of the two, the other will gracefully withdraw from the contest for her hand. Célimène enters to prepare for the visit of Arsinoé whom she viciously criticizes for being prudish and for being in love with Alceste. Nevertheless, when Arsinoé comes into the room, Célimène flatters her and pretends to welcome the visit. The two gentlemen, laughing at the false manners of Célimène, leave. Arsinoé explains without delay the reasons for her coming: as a true friend, she wishes to inform Célimène about the gossip she has been overhearing. Célimène has been the topic of conversation because of the excessive number of visitors she receives and conspicuous ways, especially the flirtations. Of course, Arsinoé claims that she has defended Célimène. Nevertheless, Célimène is advised to change her way of life at once if she wishes to remain in good standing within social circles. When Célimène has her turn to speak, she repeats what she has supposedly overheard about Arsinoé's excessive prudery. She enumerates in detail all the many faults of Arsinoé. The general criticism of society is that Arsinoé should improve herself first before she embarks upon a crusade to attack and reform others. Arsinoé claims in defense that her remarks have so hurt Célimène that the latter resorts to these slanders. Age is the cause for Arsinoé's jealousy, according to Célimène, and the increasing bitterness at seeing suitors ignore her. Every woman could have admirers if they behaved like Célimène; men flock around her because of her flirtatious and indecent conduct. The conversation rapidly leads to more and more sarcastic and angry remarks until the arrival of Alceste gives Célimène an excuse to leave Arsinoé.

Arsinoé welcomes Alceste and flatters him to a high degree. Because of his merit, he should be more recognized by the Court. Alceste states bluntly that merit, if it is true merit, is its own lawyer; he feels that no exceptional effort or service has been performed for the nation. He cannot use doubletalk but must be sincere in all his ways. She tries to tempt him by referring to influential persons who could aid his rise to power. Even if a position were obtained for him, Alceste knows that his sincerity would cause him to lose it in a short time. Arsinoé finally warns him against Célimène: his love is wasted because Célimène is unfaithful and he should seek a more loyal woman. She is of course trying to woo Alceste which fact he somewhat suspects. When asked to present proof of Célimène's betrayal of his affections, Arsinoé invites Alceste to accompany her to her home.

ACT IV

Philinte and Éliante are discussing the case in the Court between Alceste and Oronte. Alceste refused to withdraw any of his remarks and regretted that he felt compelled to speak the truth. He is sorry that he could not have said that the **sonnet** was better. Éliante admires Alceste for this quality of sincerity, and it is evident that she is in love with him. But Philinte is puzzled by his honesty and directness which has not detected the truth about Célimène and which has ignored these forthright traits in Éliante. Éliante will do nothing to oppose the affair between Alceste and Célimène; however, she admits that if the two stopped loving each other, she would accept Alceste as her husband. Philinte then declares his love for Éliante and his hopes that if Alceste and Célimène marry, he can have Éliante as his wife. Nevertheless, Éliante makes clear that she does not love Philinte.

Alceste enters at this decisive moment with the news that he has the proof that Célimène has indeed deceived him and with none other than rival whom he thought less of, Oronte. By means of a letter, he claims, he has understood the deceitful nature of Célimène. In order to secure revenge, he asks Éliante to marry him, but she tries to soothe him by advising more thought about Célimène's actions. When Célimène approaches, Éliante and Philinte leave so that the two lovers can be alone and settle their differences. Without delay, Alceste irrationally accuses Célimène, in very biting and sarcastic tones, of treason. She pretends ignorance of his accusations, and Alceste is forced to produce the letter. As the letter is unsigned, Célimène could have denied she wrote it; however, she admits her authorship but reveals that it could have been to a woman. There is no mention of Oronte's name or any other man's name; Alceste admits he was told that Oronte was the recipient.

The tables begin to be turned when Célimène now refuses to deny she wrote the letter to Oronte, and Alceste pleads for an explanation, innocent enough to calm his wild jealousy. Célimène notes this weakness on his part and attacks his lack of faith in her love; his lov is too extreme for her. Alceste begs that his love is based on the desire for complete acceptance.

At this point, Alceste's servant, Du Bois, comes to report very bad news: a messenger has delivered legal papers and one of Alceste's friends has written a note urging him to flee the city. Alceste, thoroughly alarmed, leaves in haste.

ACT V

Alceste confides to Philinte that he intends to abandon society; all his enemies have combined against him to bring about the loss of his lawsuit. Every point of honor and justice has been violated by his foes in this effort. He is even in danger of being placed under arrest because of the perjury of a witness. Philinte urges an appeal in the courts but Alceste refuses, wishing to be martyr to injustice. Escape is no solution, and one must stay to fight wrongs by the moderate and delicate exercise of philosophy, replies Philinte. He offers to bring Éliante downstairs to encourage Alceste.

Alceste remains in a darkened corner of the room; he can overhear the conversation between Célimène and Oronte who come in. Oronte demands that Célimène choose between himself and Alceste, and the latter emerges from the shadows to agree with Oronte. Célimène believes that such a choice should not be made in public; these very intimate matters call for concealment of the decision from the disappointed lover. Éliante, Acaste, Clitandre, and Arsinoé join the discussion and demand from Célimène an explanation for the unsigned letter. All her suitors are discussed scornfully in the letter and all of them now reject Célimène for the revelation of her insulting remarks. Arsinoé hopes that Alceste will now court her, but his refusal then turns her against him. After the departure of the angry gentlemen, Célimène admits to Alceste that she has wronged him; her behavior has earned her social disapproval with new enemies ready to ruin her. In order to redeem herself and live according to the high principles he has long urged, Célimène is urged to flee from society with Alceste. They will dwell in solitude and live in peace with their love. Célimène is unable to renounce the world at so early an age, and Alceste at last realizes that she does not love him. If true love existed, she would be prepared to make this sacrifice. When Célimène departs, Alceste turns to Éliante and Philinte whom he recognizes as suited to each other. Determined to live the life of a hermit. away from society and faithful to his high aims, he exits.

Comment

The Misanthrope (Le Misanthrope), in verse, did not enjoy great success when it was first performed, and the reasons may be found in some measure in the dramatic changes from Molière's other comedies and in the dramatist's private life. The second argument is more difficult to prove, yet it is undeniable that Molière saw sorrow mounting by 1666. He had lost his first child, the marital woes with Armande Béjart were increasing, and his health was beginning to fail because of the hectic life he had to lead. Beyond a doubt, the attacks and plots of his many enemies were becoming more annoying. Within the play itself, Molière abandoned his former comic manner, and there are few hearty laughs for the audience. The humor is in the drama but it is an intellectual and philosophical humor. The play is directed to a better educated and more intelligent theater than are other works. Perhaps for these causes, the comedy has been hotly debated and criticized. Jean-Jacques Rousseau, the French philosopher of the eighteenth century, severely condemned *The Misanthrope* for praising evil and downgrading goodness; André Gide, the French novelist and Nobel Prize winner of this century, confessed himself very disturbed by the play; and George Eliot, the English novelist of the nineteenth century, called it "the foremost and most complete production of its kind in the world."

Besides the absence of the comical and humorous, even farcical, traits, so common and so characteristic of Molière, *The Misanthrope* has deep and complicated views on life and society. The philosophy is contradictory, and Molière never clearly indicates his own outlook. The dialogue between the characters must be reviewed and reflected upon; consequently, the play lacks the dynamic quality of other plays. The plot is very weak, and there is little action to sustain interest for the viewer. Speeches are lengthy, and the characters resemble lawyers opposing one another by argument and counter-argument. It is curious to note that Molière never returned to the type of comedy of *The Misanthrope*.

The play is a psychological study in its concentration on the person of Alceste, and it is likewise a play of manners in the society of Louis XIV. This is the one play above all in which the hero dominates the story from the beginning; he is always in the center of the action. The problem that Molière creates is that of the individual within society, and yet, surprisingly enough, the play did not arouse the fury which other works, such as Tartuffe, did. The importance of *The Misanthrope* is in the universal quality of the play. It creates a situation which exists in all groups at all times. There are not the particular problems of other plays, such as marriage, the rights of children, the duties of parents, and the ambitions of the middle class.

What Molière lost in dramatic value within the drama, he gained in the depth of penetration into character and the profundity of language. The speeches are models of debate exercises, and the characters display many facets of their particular moods. One cannot completely fathom the mysterious character of Alceste or be sure of Molière's point of view in this masterpiece; perhaps this is one of the reasons why it is ranked as the high point in his theatrical art. It is a play which demands excellent actors, not in the obviously comic, but in the nuances and tones of speech and manner which can lend more than mere interpretation of the meaning to the viewer. Of all Molière's plays, it is probably the most difficult to read.

THE MISANTHROPE

CHARACTER ANALYSES

ALCESTE

Molière adapted the name of his principal character from the Greek for a strong, forcefull, and domineering person. Throughout the play, Alceste places great emphasis upon the self; for example, he stresses the fact that "I" want this or that. Never does he offer to admit he may be wrong; never does he consent to a possible compromise. Therefore, he fails to achieve any of his goals and ideals. On the contrary, he alienates everyone with whom he comes into contact; indeed, it may be said that society is perhaps somewhat worse at the conclusion of the drama. Alceste has been called the "Hamlet" of Molière if one can accept the designation of the French dramatist as France's Shakespeare. Alceste also has been compared to *Don Quixote* as portrayed by the Spanish novelist, Cervantes. It may be recalled how in one **episode** Don Quixote refused to listen to the advice and warnings of his servant, Sancho Panza, and attacked windmills which he insisted were giants. In *The Misanthrope*, Alceste is constantly admonished and advised by Philinte.

Alceste is the most profound and philosophical of the theatrical characters created by Molière. He is both tragic and comic, and the play is both a tragedy and a comedy. However, most critics would assign more importance to the concept that it is still primarily a comedy. Beyond a doubt, the audience does not encounter the abundance of humor in the situation of Alceste as in other figures of Molière's theater, but Alceste, by being so serious, so rigid, so dogmatic, and, in essence, so lacking in humanity, is laughable. The high point of Alceste's removal from reality is found in the scene of the **sonnet**; from that point on, he is doomed by his own actions, too rash and too ridiculous. One laughs instead of crying or pitying when he makes his final exit.

PHILINTE

As in so many of his works, Molière inserts a figure of good sense and reason, but Philinte is more than all this: he is an honest, upright, and loyal friend. Alceste, in his overpowering ambition to make society better, overlooked an example of high principles in a person usually near him. Of course, he is not perfect if Alceste's views are followed: Philinte antagonizes no one, and his attitudes are generally mild and not very controversial. He seeks to survive in a society and perhaps improve it a little, although he is not too optimistic on this issue. At the end, Philinte is the only one of the players who has triumphed; he has won Aliante, even though it may have been by default and as a second choice.

ORONTE, ACASTE, CLITANDRE

These three gentlemen of the Court represent "high society" of the time of Louis XIV; they are closely in agreement on manners and customs of the nobility. In the characters, reality and appearance can be observed at close hand: on the surface, they are polished courtiers with all the advantages and privileges of the aristocracy; underneath the glitter, they are unworthy leaders and men of influence in France. manners had become more refined and morals had degenerated, Molière seems to say. While it is not possible to state that Molière intends a broad and devastating criticism of society, it is quite obvious that he was criticizing the social circles around the king.

CÉLIMÈNE, ÉLIANTE, ARSINOÉ

Célimène and Arisonoe complement each other in various ways; they are both rivals for an important place in society and seek to destroy each other. In the long, bitter scene of the confrontation, the two women employ different techniques to secure their goals, but both make use of slander, gossip, and insults very freely. Célimène is bold and flirtatious whereas Arsinoé plays prude. Éliante, while she belongs to the same class as the other women, is most sincere ad honest of the members of the Court potrayed in *The Misanthrope.* For this reason, Philinte counseled Alceste to court her instead of Célimène. Éliante, who maintain some honorable standards of ethics, still manages to keep on amicable terms with the others and finds a husband in Philinte, although it should be recalled that she originally rejected him.

THE MISANTHROPE

ESSAY QUESTIONS AND ANSWERS

Question: What are the virtues and vices which Molière outlines in *The Misanthrope?*

Answer: One must keep in mind that Molière is no revolutionary nor is he even a mild social reformer. Molière is first of all an observer of life and next a man who contemplates what he has noticed, and finally looks with a smile upon the virtues and vices of man and society. The problem of the role of the individual within the social circle has already been noted. Alceste does nothing to pacify or to improve the condition of the Court about which he is so furious. On the contrary, his influence is brought to nothing, there is no amelioration, and he himself goes off to solitude. He has given up the struggle, defeated by his own domineering will unchecked by reason.

Molière speaks well of friendship and love in *The Misanthrope.* Only through communication on rational terms can society continue to function; thus the dramatist wishes groups to converse and to behave moderately. Friendship is a more difficult quality to be had; acquaintances abound and these contacts must be kept, but the art of making a friend and keeping that friend is highly complicated. Philinte suffers much from Alceste, and the latter even dismisses him at the end of the Act I. Friendship can never blossom from the false attitudes of Célimène and Arsinoé, nor from the gentlemen of the Court, Oronte and Acaste. The two moderate members, Philinte and Éliante, have many acquaintances and achieve some good from adhering to these groups. Friendship, nevertheless, only develops when two comparable individuals meet; this genial situation is seen in the relationship between Philinte and Éliante. Just as friendship comes slowly, so also will love come about from friendship. Éliante spurned Philinte at the beginning of Act IV, but they are paired at the play's end. Courtesy, good manners, and gentleness are also virtues in Molière's play. These virtues could be vices, however, if they hid hypocritical and false men and women. Yet they cannot be put aside because they are misused. The virtues of calmness and humility are part of the legacy of reason, common sense, and moderation. Molière is sketching a portrait of the man of society, the courtier and adviser of the king, who brings virtue to bear, if at all, through good example and talent, modestly displayed.

The vices in *The Misanthrope* are naturally the failure to follow the virtues outlined above, but they are also the immoderate use of the qualities. Virtue becomes vice when the will is supreme. Virtue is not its own reward and justification; there is a social function and purpose in the application of virtues. When man and society are disrupted by the virtues run rampant and become vices, then these attributes are ridiculous and ludicrous. Of course, there are also outright vices detailed in *The Misanthrope*. Slander, bribery, perjury, etc., are used to defeat Alceste in the lawsuit. When justice can be subverted, a social organization is in severe trouble. The result of the flouting of vices, such as the above, by the leading members of the nation is nothing short of disastrous for everyone. These vices are the most obvious and evil, but there is also the vice of hypocrisy under the guise of politeness. Célimène is caught in this trap when the letter is produced in which she ridiculed all her male friends; she is left without friends and even acquaintances.

Thus in Molière the virtues are depicted gently and tactfully; vices are painted subtly but surely; and the main emphasis is centered on the danger of virtue being converted into vice by lack of understanding. It may be seen in consequence why this play is the most controversial and most philosophical drama in the theater of Molière.

Question: What is the problem of idealism and **realism** in *The Misanthrope?*

Answer: *The Misanthrope* ends on an incomplete note: it is neither comedy nor tradegy; the **themes** of **realism** and idealism have not been reconciled. Alceste is so far removed from the real nature of existence that he retreats into the wasteland of his own exalted idealism. Célimène admits the reality of her situation and that of society without endeavoring in any way to apply ideals to some improvement. Oronte inhabits an equally shallow world of pretense and falsehood. Only Cléante attempts some union of the ideal and the real but it is in respects no more than a weak compromise. According to Éliante, the individual may be able to achieve the transformation of some ideals into the real world; however, his efforts must never be too forceful or too emphatic. If he fails, then he should not be too concerned. There is in *The Misanthrope* the problem of idealism and **realism** regarding relations between persons and society. Idealism is defeated but the audience suffers no distress at the failure of such lofty aims so far above the reach of the common man. Nor is **realism** a desired solution; it has too many characteristics of cynicism and hypocrisy. Thus, Molière employs the technique of a moral dilemma instead of the usual happy solution of the ramifications of plot situations.

Question: Brander Matthews has written that in *The Misanthrope*, Molière presents a portrait of the "best society of his time." Discuss this viewpoint.

Answer: In Tartuffe and in most other plays, Molière depicted the middle class and the problems facing this new social class in the seventeenth century. However, in *The Misanthrope*, he draws his characters from the aristocracy exclusively; this may be one of the reasons the play achieved little popularity during his lifetime and yet incurred the wrath of the nobility. The nobles portrayed admit they are close to the king and have influence over Louis XIV. If these individuals represent the "best society" of the day, then the French historian of the nineteenth century, Hippolyte Taine, was correct in calling upon Molière so often as a witness of the national decadence. Manners had improved; morals had declined. Literary taste had become increasingly complex and removed from reality; the implications of the fine speeches are often bitter and more insulting than those of the commoners. For example, Célimène and Arsinoé insult each other cruelly and in a fashion that the peasants would not employ. However, their tone is always formal and polished. The nobles brutally degrade Célimène in her own home when they read aloud a personal letter. Perhaps the full import of Molière's harsh analysis of his national leaders was lost on contemporary audiences; thus, the term "best society" is used ironically to characterize the cast of *The Misanthrope*.

THE MISER

THE PLAY

CHARACTERS

Harpagon Élise, his daughter Cléante, his son Valère, Harpagon's steward Mariane La Flèche, Cléante's valet Anselme Master Simon Frosine Master Jacques, Dame Claude, La Merluche, Brindavoine-servants of Harpagon Police commissioner

SETTING

Harpagon's house.

ACT I

Valère and Élise are secretly meeting to try to solve their dangerous plight. Valère, in love with Élise, has had himself introduced into her father's house as a steward so that he can be near her. Surely, as he pleads, this is proof of his love for her. She knows that he loves her but the fear of Harpagon is so great that her worries may make suspicions and jealousies grow in her mind. Valère answers all her inquiries and seeks to calm the gnawing anxieties she has.

Élise admits her gratitude also to Valère for saving her from drowning, but she has grave doubts whether they will continue their present relationship for long without being detected. As a result of his position with Harpagon, Valère feels quite safe until he can receive word of his family, thereby establishing his legitimate claim to Élise. She advises him to make an ally of her brother, but Valère fears that the strained relations between Harpagon and Cléante would endanger his cause. It would be better for Élise to discuss the situation with her brother. After Valère's departure, Cléante comes to confide in his sister that he is in love with Mariane, a girl who has recently moved into their neighborhood. The scene is very ironic: Cléante realizes his sister, not being in love, cannot understand his anguish; and she does not comprehend the consequent difficulties with Harpagon.

Both lovers of the brother and sister are not rich, and Harpagon will not release Cléante's and Élise's property until they attain a certain age. There is a bitter attack on avarice, the undue control of parents over children, and the emphasis upon a dowry as the requisite for marriage. At last, Cléante states that if he fails to borrow the money he is seeking, both of them should run away. When Harpagon and La Flèche, Cléante's valet, draw near, they disappear. These two are quarreling angrily: Harpagon suspects that La Flèche is a spy and covets his money. La Flèche answers impertinently and constantly so that Harpagon orders him from the house. Before leaving, La Flèche is searched by Harpagon to make sure he has not robbed anything. These insults make La Flèche bolder and bolder: he now wants to rob Harpagon and uses the words "miser" and "avarice" freely.

Alone, Harpagon worries whether he did the right thing by burying gold in the garden; however, he is startled to notice his children nearby. Harpagon pleads to the two children to be less extravagant, asserting that he is not wealthy. He scolds Cléante very severely for aping the aristocracy in his lavish wardrobe; he wants the son to save his money and to become a middle class citizen in all ways as he is. Since a quarrel is rapidly developing between father and son, the subject is changed to marriage-exactly the topic which Élise and Cléante want to settle. When the father inquires about his opinions regarding Mariane as a wife. Cléante is completely elated. He praises her to the skies and convinces his father that the dowry is not that important because of her outstanding merits. The blow falls when Harpagon announces that he is therefore going to marry Mariane. Cléante rushes from the room in consternation.

Élise and Harpagon then debate his plans: she is to marry Anselme this evening which she refuses to do. They denounce each other as unworthy parent and child. As Valère approaches, Harpagon offers to submit the decision to him, and Élise agrees enthusiastically. However, her enthusiasm vanishes when Valère, unsuspecting the matter at hand and seeking to ingratiate himself more into Harpagon's favor, affirms that he supports the father's position without even hearing it beforehand. When Harpagon reveals the marriage plans of Élise and Anselme, the unfortunate Valère tries to change opinions with little success; Harpagon replies to each objection of Valère, "Without a dowry!" Money must be the key to marriage arrangements; no other considerations count. At this moment of defeat for the lovers, Harpagon hears a dog barking in the garden and, fearful for his money, runs out. Valère explains to Élise that she must seek a delay for the marriage and he will continue to flatter Harpagon. Upon his return, Harpagon is convinced that Valère is working to his advantage; in fact, he leaves Élise in Valère's complete charge as he leaves the house on some business.

ACT II

Cléante and La Flèche are debating the terms of the loan which Cléante is attempting to negotiate. A middleman, Master Simon, is in contact with the lender, and it now develops that the interest rate will be twenty-five percent. There are other complications in the transaction; for example, Valère must take part of the sum in furniture and household goods instead of in cash. La Flèche pities Cléante and repeats his wish to rob Harpagon for his stinginess; Cléante comments on the way fathers hold a monetary club over the heads of their children. Cléante also explains to La Flèche's astonishment about his father's marriage proposal to Mariane. Harpagon and Master Simon enter and discuss a loan which the former is going to make. Then, La Flèche recognizes the middleman, and all four participants come to the front of the stage for the revelation of the proposed loan. Harpagon accuses his son of shameful extravagances, and the son accuses his father of shameful usury. The others run away. After an angry scene, Cléante departs; Harpagon runs into the garden to have another peek at his hidden treasure.

Frosine and La Flèche probe each other's intentions and opinions of Harpagon. Frosine hints that she is going to receive some money from the master for work she is engaged in. La Flèche doubts whether Harpagon will part with any of his cash. He denounces Harpagon so harshly that it becomes very apparent there is hatred in his heart for the master. However, he hastens away when Harpagon returns from the garden. Frosine flatters her master about his youthful appearance and predicts a long life for him. She happily confides in him that her efforts on his behalf have been successful: Mariane's mother consents to the signing of the marriage contract this very evening at his home. Harpagon is happy for another reason too: he can save money on the cost of the meal since he has invited Anselme to come at the same time. Nevertheless, Harpagon tells Frosine to persuade Mariane's mother about some dowry. Frosine counterclaims by asserting that Mariane is worth a good amount of money by dint of her way of life. Mariane does not spend much money on food, clothes, jewelry, or gambling. Thus the girl is worth much cash by her habits. Unconvinced by this peculiar logic, Harpagon still insists that a token dowry be sought from the mother. Perhaps Mariane will receive some property in the future, replies Frosine. There is another matter troubling Harpagon: he is afraid that Mariane will not like to marry an older man of his age. Frosine lies again by claiming that Mariane scorns younger men and that her descriptions of Harpagon have won the girl's heart. Thinking the moment opportune, Frosine requests a little money for a lawsuit she is engaged in from Harpagon; he is so overjoyed at his apparent winning of Mariane that he ignores the pleas of Frosine. Upon his departure, Frosine curses him but intends to keep after him for money; after all, she can go over to the other side and gain a reward.

ACT III

The preparations for the dinner in the evening are in full swing as Harpagon instructs all his servants about their duties. Of course, their most important duty is to keep costs down as much as possible. For example, furniture is not to be polished too hard; glasses are to be refilled only by request; and the servants are to conceal their soiled and worn outfits as adroitly as possible. He likewise demands respect, courtesy, and obedience from the children. Master Jacques is the last to receive instructions; he changes clothes from coachman to cook for these orders.

If money in sufficient amount is provided, Master Jacques assures the master that a wonderful meal will be served. At the mention of the word "money," Harpagon cringes and seeks the support of Valère. There occurs a very comical scene in which Valère mockingly aids Harpagon in his plans with Master Jacques; the cook opposes each suggestion of economy on Harpagon's part; and Harpagon becomes increasingly uneasy about the bills for dinner. At last, Harpagon leaves the whole affair in Valère's hands. As Harpagon commences to issue commands about the coach and horses, Master Jacques changes back into the clothes of the coachman. He refuses to drive the horses unless they are fed, and Harpagon arranges to have a neighbor do this chore.

Valère and Master Jacques finally argue to the breaking point, and Master Jacques, out of love for his master, warns Harpagon that Valère is tricking him and that he is becoming the butt of jokes by the neighborhood. When pressed to tell the stories and assured that the reports will be welcome, Master Jacques repeats many humorous incidents of Harpagon's stinginess. His reward is to be beaten by the furious Harpagon. Valère and Master Jacques quarrel anew, and the former beats the servant for his boldness. Master Jacques vows never to tell the truth again and also to seek vengeance against Valère.

Frosine and Mariane enter for the meeting with Harpagon. Mariane is in love with an unknown young man and therefore is not anxious to meet Harpagon, but Frosine urges her to be practical. Most young men are poor, and marriage with an older man will bring a sufficient inheritance upon his death to marry a younger spouse the second time. However, Mariane is shocked at the first sight of Harpagon and tells her unpleasant reactions in a whisper to Frosine. When Harpagon wishes to know what Mariane says, Frosine relates the contrary thought. Élise greets Mariane very politely, but Cléante, angered at the approaching marriage, speaks out bluntly against the plans of his father. Mariane assents to his objections to the marriage, and Harpagon experiences difficulties in separating the two young people; they begin to exchange loving words whose importance he misses.

Cléante has played a very expensive trick on his father: he has ordered very costly dishes for the dinner. Also, he shows Mariane a diamond on his father's finger, removes the stone, and offers it as a gift to her. Harpagon becomes infuriated at his son's action; an angry undertone of rage on his part and mockery on Cléante's is interrupted by the announcement of a visitor. Harpagon refuses to see anyone at this critical moment until he is told the stranger brings him money. He then hastens out, and Cléante prepares to escort Mariane to the garden. Harpagon curses his son and urges Valère to watch out for his interests.

ACT IV

Élise, Cléante, Mariane, and Frosine, now in league with the opposition against Harpagon, debate their next moves. Élise pleads with Frosine to think of some trick or maneuver against Harpagon; and the lovers, Cléante and Mariane, face the problem of duty versus love. Finally Frosine thinks of disguising herself as a wealthy lady from the provinces who wants to marry Harpagon. Frosine also has to win over Mariane's mother to the new match with Cléante. Harpagon interrupts the plotters and suspects that Cléante may have designs upon Mariane from the way he kisses her hand. Therefore he refuses to have the son accompany the group out. Harpagon now tricks Cléante: after asking the young man his opinion of Mariane whom the son pretends to downgrade as a wife, the father says that he has changed his mind and has intended her as Cléante's bride.

However, the boy's analysis is so unfavorable that he withdraws the offer. Instead, he will adhere to original plans and marry Mariane.

It is impossible for Cléante to guard his secret any longer: he admits to Harpagon that he has been in love with Mariane for some time and wants to marry her. Elated at disclosure of the secret, Harpagon forces a confrontation with his son. Cléante will have to obey his father, cease courting Mariane, and marry the woman whom Harpagon has selected for him. The implied threat is of course that of disinheritance from the estate. Cléante refuses to renounce Mariane and harsh words ensue so that Harpagon is prepared to beat his son with a stick. Master Jacques intervenes at the start of this domestic mishap and negotiates a temporary truce by misinterpreting the intentions of one to the other. The result is that both father and son believe the other has given up Mariane in his favor. In return for his help, Master Jacques holds out his hands to Harpagon for a reward but receives instead of money the promise of remembrance on the old man's part. After he leaves, the truth is learned by Harpagon and Cléante, and the fight resumes more furiously than previously. In fact, Harpagon dismisses him and disowns Cléante as his son and heir.

When Harpagon goes away, La Flèche comes up to Cléante with the news that he has found Harpagon's hidden treasure; he brings a casket under his arm to prove the story. They flee, and Harpagon returns in anguish. He renders a pitiful soliloquy in which he moans the loss of the buried gold. His tone reveals that he is now almost insane from grief and is completely suspicious of everyone and everything. He is unable to order his thoughts coherently. If he cannot hang the whole world, at fault for his loss, he will hang himself.

ACT V

Harpagon and the police commissioner are trying to get to the bottom of the theft. The latter attempts to reason with the old man in order to get at the facts, but Harpagon wants immediate action and revenge against the whole neighborhood, now converted into his enemies by his rage. The first person to be questioned is Master Jacques. Completely confused by the indirect questions, Master Jacques at first believes they are quizzing him about the coming dinner. Only the restraint and reasonable attitude of the commissioner hold back Harpagon in his quest for revenge on everyone under suspicion. When Jacques at last realizes what is going on, he seizes upon the chance to get even with Valère and accuses him of the robbery. Jacques plays on Harpagon's anxiety in a humorous manner by having him reveal details of the incident and then stating that Valère fits the description of the thief. When Valère is brought in, Harpagon accuses him of the crime in such a manner that the young man thinks the father refers to his love affair with Élise. Therefore he admits his supposed crime. In a very long scene of mistaken identity, the agony of Harpagon is laid bare: he is so upset and disturbed by the loss of the money that he cannot think clearly; all the world is interpreted in terms of the cashbox. At last, Harpagon orders Valère's arrest despite the latter's please that he belongs to a higher station in life.

Élise pleads for Valère; she asks gratitude to Valère from Harpagon for having save her life from drowning, but the father now sees no merit in the saving of his child. Anselme comes in for the dinner and the signing of the marriage contract; he does not wish to marry anyone who does not want him, but Harpagon's interests and agreements must be honored. Valère insists that he is of honorable birth and mentions that the whole city of

Naples will testify to that effect. Anselme warns the young man that he knows everything and everyone in Naples; Anselme will detect any falsehoods.

The solution of the play comes swiftly and with undue emphasis upon coincidence. Anselme reveals himself as the longlost father of Valère; and Mariane understands that she is the sister of Valère. Anselme is overjoyed at being reunited with his wife, Mariane's mother, and the two children after so many years. Harpagon still demands the return of his stolen money and holds Anselme responsible for repayment. Cléante enters with the choice for his father: he knows where the money is and will tell the hiding place in exchange for Mariane as his wife. After being assured that everything in the cashbox is intact, Harpagon readily gives his approval to this arrangement. He drives a hard bargain to the very end, and Anselme pays all the expenses of the commissioner and the coming marriage of Mariane to Cléante. Master Jacques is shown final ingratitude by his master as the cause of Harpagon's trouble. As the others leave happily, Harpagon goes out to console himself with his money.

Comment

The Miser (L'Avare), in prose, represented an important innovation in the comedy for Molière: comic and tragic plays in five acts at this time were written in verse. Dramas in one or three acts of minor value were composed in prose. For example, Molière wrote his most profound and most philosophical play, *The Misanthrope,* two years previously, in five acts in verse. *The Miser* is also about the longest comedy in the repertory of Molière. Thus, to say that he wrote the work in prose because of haste would seem to be weak explanation of this major change in the structure of Molière's theater.

However, it must be admitted that *The Miser* is easily traced to Plautus' *Aulularia*. Of course, one must recall again that Molière had received in his youth a very sound education in the classics and consequently knew the plays of Plautus, the Roman dramatist of Latin literature. In many ways, it is interesting to identify the source of *The Miser* because the genius of Molière can be determined to greater advantage. While influence exists, it is not imitation. In Plautus the emphasis is upon the plot with its various intrigues and the humor is coarse; Molière has transformed *The Miser* into a character study with wry observations upon society. On the contrary, Molière sacrifices a well-knit plot to the advantages of character delineation; the ending of *The Miser* is clearly contrived and unmotivated. There are too many uses of coincidences, dualities, and confused identities. The action is too lengthened, and the comings and goings of the actors too frequent. However, he has ably employed comic scenes to support his thesis of the problem of avarice and a miser.

The Miser did not become an immediate hit with the Parisian audiences of Molière's day; later, the assets of the comedy were recognized, and it is now performed often with the role of Harpagon desired by many French actors. Perhaps the reason for the initial coolness of viewers is found in the tragic quality already noted. Certainly there is a somber aspect in the play besides the interpretation of Harpagon as possessing tragic features. *The Miser* is an amusing play first of all, but there are many problems hinted at in this play which have not been observed so clearly before in Molière. The dramatist was entering the last phase of his life; his success was apparent, but many personal issues appear to have clouded his dramatic art. Actually, this more serious side adds depth and variety to the comedies. In *The Miser,* one encounters the heart-rending agony of family strife between father and son; the pitiful desire of an old man to find marital happiness with a very young bride; the inferior status of daughters in a household; and the hardness of a social system based on rank giving place to one judged on money. There are likewise the small difficulties of life: the need on Frosine's part for money to continue litigation, and the uncertainties of a servant's life as illustrated by Master Jacques.

THE MISER

CHARACTER ANALYSES

HARPAGON

This miser is the dominating figure of the entire comedy; all the characters and all the actions revolve about the portrayal of Harpagon. Harpagon must be interpreted on two levels: the humorous and tragic. Of course, he is primarily a comical character as his personality deteriorates because of the obsession with money. His stinginess is depicted in dealings with servants, household expenses, and his own children. His prancings about the stage are ridiculous; for example, he is obsessed about blowing out candles in the room. One of the most amusing **episodes** occurs in the third act when he is giving instructions for the dinner party that evening. However, it is interesting to remember that Harpagon fools no one; even the neighbors are well aware of his miserly personality. Of course, the children and the servants confront him directly with his vice of avarice.

Is Harpagon conscious of the vice of miserliness? The reader should be prepared to compare him with other famous misers of literature; for example, he should refer to the miser in Silas Marner by George Eliot and to Shylock in Shakespeare's *The Merchant of Venice*. Goethe, the German author of Faust and one of the leading figures of European Romanticism in the nineteenth century, saw in Harpagon a tragic side. It would not seem possible that Harpagon is fully aware of the ridiculous mannerisms he employs; for instance, he cannot sustain a conversation for long without casting glances at the garden where he has buried his gold. Since he has wanted so desperately to conceal this treasure, his gestures obviously call attention to the hiding place; thus La Flèche is able to steal the cashbox without trouble. At the same time, Harpagon is so dominated by avarice that he no longer cares what the rest of the world thinks about him. When the comedy ends, he is alone on the stage; even his children have left him to begin new lives. He thinks he is happy; in reality, he is more than laughable-he is to be pitied and ignored.

Harpagon has not only destroyed his own happiness; he has likewise lost the respect of the outside world and his servants. Of more consequence, he has almost ruined the future bliss of Élise and Cléante; it is certain that the reconciliation at the play's conclusion is no more than superficial. The parental and filial bonds have been broken forever; at a critical moment, Harpagon was tried and found wanting. Therefore, Harpagon, on the surface a highly humorous portrait of the miser and usurer, is a sad person and a dangerous member of the family group. He is dangerous because he is ready to have society collapse to regain his wealth; for example, he insists that the commissioner arrest Valère, is ready to have neighbors and servants imprisoned, and mistreats Master Jacques, the most loyal of his household, at the last curtain.

| CLÉANTE, ÉLISE |

The two children illustrate a common principle in the theatrical art of Molière: youthfulness, zest, and rebellion opposed to parental control and discipline. By far, Cléante is the more rebellious; the break with Harpagon is never concealed, and hatred, rather than mere quarrels and disagreements, is seen in their dealings. At the same time, Cléante is not the perfect son; Harpagon corrects him, one feels with reason, about his extravagances and his gambling. Surely the middle class audience of Molière's day applauded Harpagon's complaints about the expensive and impractical clothes of the nobility, and they must have appreciated likewise his admonitions not to imitate the playboy extravagances of the indolent aristocracy. Beyond a doubt, the viewer feels more sympathy than antagonism towards Cléante in his desire to share the mother's estate and marry the girl of his choice. However, Cléante, like his father, is stubborn and strongwilled; he never offers to compromise and irritates the parent beyond endurance. Unlike Valère, who seeks to obtain concessions through flattery, Cléante is the totally disobedient child. Élise, while opposing marriage plans, is torn between love and duty; she feels obligations to and respect for Harpagon despite his miserliness and authoritarian behavior.

| VALÈRE |

He is the most practical and astute of the characters in the comedy; his intelligence and cunning are proved in the first act by the way he has secured a position with Harpagon and has won the miser's confidence. He is the stronger of the two in the love match with Élise; without his steadfastness, she would have surrendered to Harpagon easily. Valère also represents the victim of a social system which demands money and social status as the foremost considerations in marriage.

ANSELME

He is the **deus ex machina** of the play. This Latin expression refers to the unexpected, sudden, and arbitrary solution of a plot by coincidences, identities, and lucky arrivals. However, Anselme does symbolize a counterbalance to Harpagon in his wise use of money for personal happiness and the joy of children.

MARIANE

Like Élise, she is caught in the trap of a social system which demands strict obedience from children in the form of consent to marriages settled by parents. Mariane is the victim of a middle class society which emphasizes money as the criterion of future bliss. Élise, with money, cannot marry Valère; Mariane, without money, cannot marry Cléante. However, Mariane is decidedly a minor character and plays no great role in the development and solution of the plot.

THE SERVANTS

All the members of the household of Harpagon suffer because of his avarice, and they detest and fear him because of his greed. Nevertheless, La Flèche is the servant who bears the most resentment; his scorn is converted into vengeance as he steals the master's treasure. Master Jacques bears the most sufferings: he is beaten by Harpagon when he tells the truth about the opinions of the neighbors towards the miser; and he is assaulted by Harpagon when he changes and tells lies to protect himself. The **irony** is found in his loyalty to Harpagon; he is the only one, for reasons unknown, who did not despite the old man. Frosine is the most designing and hypocritical of the servants; the rest of the household do little to conceal their feelings about Harpagon or are unable to control themselves. Frosine plays on the miser's vanity and flatters him beyond belief, and the result of her deception adds dimension to the tragic side of Harpagon's character. Nevertheless, Frosine betrays Harpagon with ease when he refuses to reward her financially for her help in winning Mariane.

THE MISER

ESSAY QUESTIONS AND ANSWERS

Question: Discuss *The Miser* from the viewpoint of a social drama.

Answer: Beyond a doubt, the first consideration of the play is that of a comedy of character; Harpagon is the center of attention and all is built around the many facets of his personality. However, Molière is also painting a picture of French middle class society of the Age of Louis XIV. There is a vast difference between the worlds presented in other plays of the dramatist; no longer does one see virtue and vice debated as in *The Misanthrope*, and the issue of sincerity and religious attitudes as in Tartuffe does not enter into the framework of *The Miser*. No matter how wrong Harpagon may be, he is still admired for his qualities of thrift and simplicity. It is true he has turned these traits into vices by undue emphasis and extreme positions; however, Molière would not have the middle class ideals turned aside for the lazy and extravagant life of the nobility. Molière may not be advocating a morality and setting up a philosophical system but he is indeed commenting on the epoch in which he lived.

How did Harpagon acquire his great wealth? This question is not answered in the play, but one may assume that it was not inherited as were aristocratic fortunes. Harpagon's training is obviously not that of a noble and yet he has aspirations of becoming a man of importance as well as of wealth. He has many servants, a coach with horses, and plans entertainments. Thus he embodies bourgeois ambitions to make money the new standard of worth. Marriages must be arranged with those of equal status; the desire to marry into the aristocracy is not yet manifest, but the intent to avoid marriage with lower classes is clearly seen. The dowry is the prime element in the middle class marriage.

In this atmosphere, love is absent. Although love may be a minor theme against avarice in *The Miser*, the motif is noted in the characters, including Harpagon. Love, which should be above and beyond the material struggles of the middle class, has been sacrificed in the social scheme. It is sad to see how Harpagon attempts to buy affection in his wooing of Mariane. Molière observes sharply the result of bourgeois virtues in the absence of love; only the young, still not at peace with the mature and hardened world of their elders, accept affection as a criterion of life.

As a social drama, *The Miser* also supplies reflections on the lending and borrowing practices of the time; both Harpagon and Cléante are suspicious as lender and borrower; and the interest rates are exorbitant, with vague and dishonest contracts part of the negotiations. The borrower, as in Cléante and Frosine, is at the mercy of the person with money. There is no charity or kindness indicated in the business dealings mentioned.

Question: What id the function of coincidence in *The Miser?*

Answer: Coincidence is of course one of the techniques of the comic art; the audience is cognizant of the real identity, listens and watches with amusement at the discomfort of the actors, and wonders how the truth will be revealed. However, in *The Miser*, there is a pattern beyond the mere use of coincidence in low comedy. Molière employed coincidence abundantly in humorous and farcical situations, as in *The School for Wives*. Here, there is the play on words such as "engagement" which both refers to the money-lending need of Cléante with Harpagon and the betrothal; the coincidence is more apparent, more in the spirit of low comedy because the son does not know his father is the usurer and vice versa. The **theme** of coincidence is basic to the solution when Anselme is introduced as the long-lost father.

The many uses of coincidence are in the tradition of low comedy so that **theme** dominates the play and is converted into high comedy. Behind the frantic maskings and unmaskings, there is the final fusion of the families, and the felicitous union of the group is achieved through this maneuver of low comedy. Harpagon's complete isolation from the happiness of his children and his friends is quite unique in Molière's theatre; he is removed not only from society as Alceste is in *The Misanthrope* and as Tartuffe is removed from influence over families, but from humanity. He remains alone with his gold coins. Beyond the exaggerated formula of low coincidences, there is the high comic art: a serious observation of man and his fate has been won by the many coincidences. Coincidence has served not only a functional purpose within the drama; it has a thematic aim which is revealed fully at the conclusion.

THE WOULD-BE GENTLEMAN

THE PLAY

CHARACTERS

Mr. Jourdain, a middle class citizen Mrs. Jourdain, his wife Lucile, his daughter Cléonte, Lucile's suitor Dorimène, a marquise Dorante, a count Nicole, Mr. Jourdain's servant Covielle, Cléonte's servant Music master, music master's pupil, dancing master, fencing master, philosophy master, merchant tailor, apprentice tailor, singers, dancers, other ballet characters.

SETTING

Mr. Jourdain's home in Paris.

ACT I

The music master and the dancing master are discussing their luck in finding such a generous patron in Mr. Jourdain. However, they both complain about his stupidity and lack of culture; they receive no artistic recognition from this employment at a commoner's home. At the same time, with the money received, they can pay their bills and maintain some semblance of social standing until they are applauded as great artists. Mr. Jourdain enters dressed in an expensive tasteless combination of trousers, jacket, and dressing gown. It is immediately apparent how ridiculous and ludicrous he behaves and looks, and the teachers can barely control their laughter. Mr. Jourdain is also ostentatious in demonstrating how he goes about with two lackeys. For example, he cannot decide to listen to a new song with greater enjoyment with the dressing gown on or off. He is not too pleased with the song, anyway and sings a rather common love song he knew. Although the teachers are horrified at his taste in music, they lavish praise upon his efforts in the hope of getting more employment. The music master and the dancing master are particularly eager to take advantage of Jourdain's efforts to climb the social ladder. To show the effects of their training, the teachers arrange a chorus and dance performance. Mr. Jourdain is bewildered and puzzled at the meaning of the performances and enjoys them only because he is supposed to do so.

ACT II

After the singing and dancing, Mr. Jourdain decides to have them performed again today for a female guest he is having. He is also advised to have a musicale in his home once a week. The dancing master attempts to teach Mr. Jourdain the minuet, and the lesson is of course poorly executed by the inexperienced middle class citizen. He likewise tries to perfect the proper bow before Dorimène, the marquise he plans to entertain. The result is naturally unsuccessful, and the fencing master's lesson rescues him. The fencing master pointedly calls attention to the importance of his art against music, dancing, and singing. The other teachers, seeing their easy money being sacrificed for a rival's gain, begin to fight with the fencing master. Although Jourdain tries to stop the quarrel, it is only through the arrival of the philosophy master that temporary peace is restored. However, he expounds upon the advantages of his profession to the point where the others realize that he is seeking to usurp their favored positions. Thus they unite to attack him. Ironically, the philosophy master, who preached reason and sweetness, fights with gusto against his enemies. Jourdain, completely bewildered at the ferocity of these men of learning and culture, is powerless to stop them. Their language degenerates also, and they show themselves to be opportunists and rather crude types.

At last, the philosophy master and Jourdain escape from the fighting and the others leave. Jourdain wishes to learn, but it is painfully apparent that he is lacking in the fundamentals of a classical education. He admits that his parents failed to educate him according to the aristocratic standards of the age. He is a thoroughly practical man and rejects the sciences of logic, ethics, and physics. Instead, he wants to learn spelling. So excited and ambitious is Jourdain that he is unaware of the pedantic manners of the philosophy master. For example, he is given the linguistic explanations for the sounds of the vowels and believes he is pronouncing them better and differently than previously. A lesson on the consonants is planned for the next day, and some preliminary, equally erudite, explanations are given by the teacher. Confiding in the philosophy master, Jourdain requests help in composing a love letter to Dorimène. A very humorous scene ensues in which Jourdain realizes that a difference exists between prose and poetry; for instance, he concludes that he has been speaking prose all his life. The composition of the first sentence of the love letter is an amusing commentary on the style of "preciosity," the flowery and complicated literary style of the age. Thinking he has made progress in learning because of the flatteries of the greedy philosophy master, Jourdain now turns his attention to the tailor.

To the accompaniment of music and the dance steps of apprentice tailors, Jourdain is dressed in a new suit in the style of the aristocracy. He fails to take action against the master tailor for making a suit for himself out of Jourdain's material. When all the tailors flatter him with titles such as "gentleman" and "my lord," the duped middle class citizen becomes generous with tips. The act ends with the performance of a dance.

ACT III

Jourdain and his two lackeys march about the stage to practice their entrance into society; he has Nicole brought in to see what effect his new suit will have on her. She laughs so uproariously that he threatens to beat her; however, she prefers to be beaten if she can continue to laugh at his ridiculous appearance. She does object to cleaning up the house after the so-called aristocratic guests of Jourdain left it in disarray. Mrs. Jourdain enters and berates her husband for his foolish behavior; she warns him that he is making himself the laughing-stock of the neighborhood. Both Nicole and Mrs. Jourdain ridicule the master for his lack of common sense and his foolish pretensions to the social graces. His wife wants him to think about marrying off the daughter and predicts that he will be whipped like a schoolboy for his conduct. In a very ironical **episode**, Jourdain endeavors to play the role of the teacher: he explains to the two women the distinction between prose and poetry, the explanations of the vowels, etc., exactly as he was just told. His reaction to their stupidity parallels that of his own instructor. However, in a fencing lesson, Nicole, unaware of the names of the thrusts, is adept at pricking Jourdain with the sword.

The quarrel between Jourdain and his wife is centered in the differences between the middle class and the nobility. The count with whom Jourdain is friendly uses him to borrow money, Mrs. Jourdain asserts. Her husband states that this money is well spent since he will be able to enter into more important social groups. Actually, Jourdain is not able to explain that the count is arranging meetings for him with the marquise. When Dorante, the count, comes in, friction among the three comes to the surface. Dorante flatters Jourdain to the sarcastic comments of Mrs. Jourdain; she is apparently proved incorrect about Dorante when he proposes to discuss his debts to her husband. After Jourdain enumerates precisely the cause and sum of each loan for a total of 15,800 francs. Dorante accepts the figure and wants it rounded off to 18,000 francs-by means of a new loan now. Jourdain is torn between the loss of additional funds and the taunts of his wife that she is right in her estimate of Dorante. At last, Jourdain goes into another room to bring Dorante the money. Dorante seeks to use flattery on Mrs. Jourdain to win her over to his side but fails.

Jourdain comes back with the loan for Dorante, and the two withdraw to another side of the room to discuss the wooing of Dorimène by the middle class citizen. Dorante, acting as the intermediary, assures Jourdain that he is having some success; the lavish expenditures of money on entertainments and presents are the best ways to win the heart of a noble lady. Mrs. Jourdain and Nicole suspect that something is very amiss in the whisperings of the two men; the servant sneaks next to Jourdain and Dorante but is boxed on the ear by Jourdain before she can overhear much of the conversation. Nevertheless, she can report that a meeting is being arranged about which Mrs. Jourdain is to know nothing. The wife suspects that another woman is involved, but she is more concerned momentarily about marriage plans of Lucile, her daughter, and Cléonte whom she approves as a husband. Nicole is equally delighted as she wants to marry Cléonte's servant, Covielle. After Mrs. Jourdain leaves, Nicole is met by Cléonte and Covielle who insult her to her great surprise. Therefore, she hastens to tell her mistress about this odd conduct. Cléonte and Covielle criticize their girl friends for the way they have been supposedly ignored. When Cléonte wishes to be told unpleasant things about Lucile and Covielle complies, he now reverses himself and defends her. Covielle is convinced that Cléonte is hopelessly in love with Lucile, but the former promises to show how he hates her when they meet.

At the entrance of the girls, the master and servant stand firm and refuse to discuss the apparent snubs of the morning until Lucile and Nicole now become stubborn. It is the men's turn to follow the girls around the stage, begging and pleading. Disgusted at the cool reception, the men plan to leave and the girls yield at this possibly fatal moment. The explanation is simple: an old aunt whom they had to please was with them in the morning and therefore they had to ignore the lovers. Mrs. Jourdain hastens in to tell Cléonte to ask her husband, now approaching, for Lucile's hand. Jourdain is interested in only one question: is Cléonte a gentleman? Cléonte answers brilliantly that he cannot lie and conceal his origin; he has served well in the army and is from a good family, but he is not of noble birth. When Jourdain refuses to allow the marriage, Mrs. Jourdain boldly attacks her husband for denying his own humble middle class background. She wants happiness for her daughter with an honorable husband instead of a titled son-in-law who may be penniless. She is likewise afraid of the dire consequences for the mother and father of a titled daughter; they will be ostracized from the society in which their daughter lives. Alone, Cléonte and Covielle debate their unfortunate plight; however, the servant gets the idea to play a trick on Jourdain with the use of a group of actors. They exit to prepare the plot; Jourdain enters, very upset about the quarrels in the family.

When he leaves to prepare himself for the guests, Dorimène and Dorante talk about their love affair. It is now revealed that Jourdain's expenditures have been spent by Dorante to advance his own wooing of Dorimène. However, he cannot yet persuade her to marry him. Jourdain enters and makes a fool of himself in bowing to Dorimène, trying to express poetic greetings, and speaking of his love for her. Dorante goes between both of them, whispering misinterpretations to help his own cause. The cooks come in with the dinner and perform a dance.

ACT IV

Dorante and Dorimène eat heartily and exchange conversations in the elaborate and complex poetic language then in vogue. Jourdain is limited to a few comments of admiration for the marquise. A chorus provides singing and music. Mrs. Jourdain spoils the party by entering and criticizing the expenses of her pretentious husband. Dorante states that he is paying for the party; nevertheless, Mrs. Jourdain denies all this and upbraids him for exploiting her husband's follies. She also insults the marquise for breaking up a family in listening to the flirtatious talk of Jourdain. Dorimène rushes from the room, and Dorante, seeing his own plans upset, follows her. Husband and wife quarrel angrily, and she departs.

Covielle, disguised in Oriental costume, comes to greet Jourdain in the name of the Grand Turk's son now in Paris.

Incredulous at first, Jourdain falls into the trap when Covielle uses the word "gentleman" in referring to Jourdain and his father. He speaks to Jourdain a mixture of Turkish, Arabic, and Hebrew and completely nonsensical words. It seems that the Grand Turk's son wants to marry Lucile and that Jourdain will be made a noble or a "mamamouchi." Delighted at this prospect, Jourdain is told the Grand Turk's son is already on the way; somewhat startled at this haste, he has to explain that Lucile is in love with Cléonte. There is no problem, Covielle assures Jourdain: the Grand Turk's son bears a remarkable resemblance to Cléonte whom he has seen. Cléonte with pages comes into the room, and Jourdain does not penetrate his disguise as the Grand Turk's son. A very humorous farce is enacted by means of ceremonious gestures and the foreign language of the "Turks." Dorante joins the group, recognizes Covielle, but agrees to fool Jourdain with the others.

Then the ceremony of making Jourdain a "mamamouchi" occurs; the colorful costumes, dancing, singing, and gestures take up the rest of the act. Jourdain, excited and pleased by this initiation ceremony, cannot probe the farcical and ludicrous aspects of what is being done to him. For example, he has to bear the weight of a Koran upon his back for a long time. The imaginary language and weird chants lend a mysterious and comical air to all the proceedings.

ACT V

After Jourdain is alone, his wife comes, but he demands respect and courtesy from her because of his new exalted rank. His behavior convinces her that Jourdain has gone mad, particularly as he dances his way out. She follows him fearfully. Dorante and Dorimène enter and agree to go on with the plot against

Jourdain. The marquise has decided to marry Dorante to stop him from spending all his money on the courting, she laughingly explains. They both feign to pay great homage to Jourdain as a "mamamouchi." Cléonte is paid the same pretended respect by the French nobles as the Grand Turk's son.

Only one problem remains for Jourdain: how to persuade Lucile to marry the Grand Turk's son. She refuses to marry him until she realizes that Cléonte is in disguise; then, she humorously assents to her father's wishes. When Mrs. Jourdain appears, she opposes the marriage to the Turkish nobleman even when Dorante and Dorimène talk in favor of it. Finally, Covielle has to take her aside, explain the disguises, and the trick played on Jourdain. The only way to bring the marriage about was to make use of Jourdain's mania for rich and noble manners of life. All ends happily with a ballet. The marriage contracts between Cléonte and Lucile, Dorante and Dorimène, Nicole and Covielle, are signed, and Jourdain is still unaware of the deception.

Comment

Dramatically and artistically, *The Would-Be Gentleman* (Le Bourgeois Gentilhomme), written in prose, has several defects. The plot is not introduced until the third act; the fourth act is purely theatrical spectacle; and there is a very weak, extremely brief last act. There is certainly no psychological probing and sparkling language as in *The Misanthrope*, Tartuffe, and *The Miser*. The first two acts repeat each other to some extent. One might expect, therefore, that this play would be regarded as a failure.

Quite the contrary, nevertheless, this comedy is one of the most popular and best-known plays in the entire repertory of

Molière. No matter how severely the critics may carp at the construction of the play, and we have seen that they have good reasons, audiences immediately accepted the play as a hit. Surely in the theater, popularity must be considered some sign of the lasting value and influence of a drama. This musical comedy was certainly the big hit of the day: Molière wrote the play at the king's suggestion to provide revenge for the monarch after a Turkish mission had snubbed him due to his inferior status in their eyes; the play was performed outside Paris at one of the king's estates at state expense; and the Parisian viewers took it to their hearts at once.

The play is sheer entertainment: ballets, music, and dancing with colorful costumes and fanciful ceremonies dazzle the spectators' eyes. All is done in the name of light entertainment; there is nothing of the serious, sad, or sarcastic in the comedy. In other words, while social criticism is apparent, the first aim of Molière has been to achieve harmony. Nothing is overdone; everything is in balance at the play's end. There are no hard feelings on the part of anyone. Even Jourdain will get over his discomfort at being the butt of some jokes. This concept of harmony is the basis of education, as can be observed in the teaching lessons; education should provide a balance between extremes of ignorance displayed by Jourdain and extremes of pedantry demonstrated by the teachers. Harmony is met again at the marriages arranged in the last act; three social classes are joined together harmoniously within their own class structures. Jourdain and his wife will continue their middle class life, the wiser for excursions into areas not their proper domain.

THE WOULD-BE GENTLEMAN

CHARACTER ANALYSES

JOURDAIN

There is nothing of the harsh or bitter in the portrayal of Jourdain on the part of Molière. Even at the play's end, when the marriages are arranged and everyone is having a good laugh at his expense, Jourdain still remains dazzled by the deceitful trick. When he finally comprehends what has happened, he will probably not take it so hard as happened with *The Miser*. Molière has not depicted any dark side to Jourdain's nature; his ambitions, while vaulting, never make unreasonable demands on his family and friends. Even Lucile's marriage is not insistently arranged, and the forceful influence of Mrs. Jourdain always cows her husband somewhat. There is no trace of the melancholy in Jourdain; he always rebounds rapidly after a setback and never broods over his inability to become a gentleman. Likewise, the tricks played on him are only humorous in nature for his own benefit.

There is a certain amount of sympathy for Jourdain in his efforts to educate himself and to gain a higher place in society. After working hard to amass a fortune and raising a family by middle class standards, he wants to enjoy the fruits of his labor. Jourdain realizes that there is a world apart from that of money. He is comical and ridiculous when he abandons exactly the qualities of common sense, shrewdness, and frugality which enabled him to become prosperous. Everything which makes him believe he is making progress is actually bringing about his downfall. Undoubtedly, the social intent of Molière is that the bourgeoisie should not ape slavishly the pedantic and extravagant world of the decadent aristocracy.

MRS. JOURDAIN

She forms an interesting counterforce to the noble aims of her husband and surprisingly enough reflects not middle class but popular origins in her speech and manners. In other words, she seems already to have taken a step up the social ladder by being a member of the middle class. Mrs. Jourdain is not the shyly protesting wife seen in other comedies of Molière; on the contrary, there are indications in the way she opposes and talks back to her husband that he is perhaps somewhat henpecked. Nevertheless, the two present a well-ordered example of the union of the lower classes and the middle class.

DORIMÈNE AND DORANTE

These two characters show the highly exaggerated manners and attitudes of the aristocracy; their snobbishness and insincerity are added to the absence of any ethical or moral codes. Dorante is the more extreme example; he is completely corrupt, has no scruples about borrowing money without repaying it, and uses everyone to his own advantage. He is one of the strongest illustrations in Molière's theater of the continuing economic decline of the aristocracy and its increasing corruption. Even at the drama's conclusion, the aristocrats despise the middle class citizens with whom they have come into contact.

COVIELLE AND NICOLE

More than a mere servant, Covielle is the mainspring of the successful plot to fool Jourdain. He organizes and arranges all the performances and keeps Jourdain off balance by his impersonation of the Turk. Cléonte and Covielle form a duo in their use of refined, delicate language and common, everyday speech, respectively. Yet they have the same thoughts about winning their respective girl friends. Covielle also comes to the rescue in the closing minutes of the comedy when he prevents Mrs. Jourdain from stopping a marriage she already wants. Nicole, while playing the female servant role corresponding to Covielle's and being in love with him, is more impertinent and frank in her remarks, especially toward her employer, Jourdain.

CLÉONTE AND LUCILE

Unlike the lovers in several other plays of Molière, they do not express the overpowering struggle and desperation of two young lovers, fighting parental control and wealth. Since the play is so completely a farce, Molière omitted these strong sentiments in the youths. On the contrary, he dwells more on the small lovers' quarrel when Cléonte was snubbed out of necessity by Lucile. Cléonte is overshadowed by the stronger personality of his servant, Covielle.

THE TEACHERS

Molière makes a very sweeping indictment of the pedantic and hypocritical teaching methods of seventeenth century France. The language of instruction is far removed from the living expression of the people so that communication is by itself a problem of the pedagogical system. There is no attempt to correlate learning with life. At the same time, the teachers are self-seeking and cynical; outwardly, they are aspiring artists who are snobbish in their choice of careers and patrons. In actuality, they are materialistic and jealous; they are motivated by financial greed and worldly success. One of the ironies of this comedy is found in the desired imitation by Jourdain of these instructors as perfect models.

THE WOULD-BE GENTLEMAN

ESSAY QUESTIONS AND ANSWERS

Question: What is the role of money in *The Would-Be Gentleman*?

Answer: Money is the dominant symbol of the play to represent the changing social background of France during the seventeenth century. Money is the great dividing line between the old, entrenched situation of the nobility and the rising ambitions of the middle class. Without money, the aristocracy sinks deeper into debt and eventual financial ruin; for example, Dorante must condescend to unethical borrowing and cheating to maintain his way of life. With money, the middle class can try to enter court circles, marry into noble families, and seek power and status. Neither the aristocracy nor the middle class can survive and grow without the aid of the other. Under the guise of a musical comedy with the aim of harmony, and the intention to entertain his public, Molière has analyzed brilliantly a problem in France which would be one of the causes for the French Revolution in 1789.

Even the arts and artists must come to the new social class, the bourgeoisie, for money to support themselves. In other words, culture will have to seek a mass audience in order to survive. It must be recalled that Molière managed a theater and knew this fact from the very beginning of his career. His early failure and bankruptcy in Paris, the years of exile in the provinces, and the box-office receipts during his entire residence in Paris taught him the need to win the sympathy - and money - of the people. Of course, the king's patronage was vital in protecting him from enemies and made good publicity for a new play, but Molière was first and foremost a popular dramatist. The problem in this new shift is obviously: how can the middle class be taught to enjoy the arts and support the artists? Again, there must be communication and harmony; art and artist must not act so snobbishly toward their new patrons Money is the great divider between the middle class and the aristocracy.

THE LEARNED LADIES

THE PLAY

CHARACTERS

Chrysale, rich middle class citizen Philaminte, his wife Armande, older daughter Henriette, younger daughter Ariste, brother of Chrysale Bélise, sister of Chrysale Clitandre, Henriette's suitor Trissotin, a scholar-pedant Vadius, a scholar Martine, a kitchen maid Lépine, servant Julien, valet of Vadius A notary

SETTING

The home of Chrysale in Paris.

ACT I

Armande and Henriette are at odds about the intention of Henriette to get married. Henriette has no great ambitions except to find love and happiness with a husband and home. Her sister makes fun of all these common ideals; she wants to become a learned lady like their mother. Armande wants to cultivate philosophy and the pleasures of the mind instead of the sensual joys of the body. Henriette is not as dogmatic as her sister; she believes that each of them has a different temperament and must live her life accordingly. The difference between the sisters is noticeable in their way of speaking: Henriette uses a simpler language while Armande employees the "precious" or complicated and exaggerated idiom of the day in France. Henriette reminds her sister that their mother possesses the present aspirations of both girls. Armande cannot compromise in her attack upon Henriette; she belittles her sister's choice of a husband, Clitandre. Armande also feels that she has a first claim on Clitandre, if she wants him at any time. She likewise asserts that he still loves her.

Upon the appearance of Clitandre, Armande asks him which of the sisters he really loves. Clitandre, without hesitation, replies that Armande so spurned his love by her attitudes that he found true love and esteem with Henriette. Angered by his rejection, Armande recalls to her sister that consent from their parents must be had. Henriette hopes that her sister will help to obtain that permission, but her sister avoids further comment by her departure. Clitandre and Henriette plan their strategy: according to Henriette, it will be better to win over her mother first since she really controls the household. Clitandre dislikes dealing with the learned ladies such as Philaminte. He wants women to appear less intellectual in front of men; he particularly dislikes Trissotin, her pedantic tutor. Clitandre attacks the whole school of pedantic and worthless writing then in great vogue; he will find it very difficult to pretend the opposite view even when the marriage to Henriette is at stake. BÉlise, Henriette's aunt, enters, and Clitandre endeavors to enlist her in his cause; she, however, is also a learned lady. In beautiful, melodic, and meaningless expressions, she concludes that Clitandre, under the guise of loving Henriette, really wants to court her. She is so removed from reality of thought by idealism of expression that Clintandre runs off in annoyance to seek help elsewhere.

ACT II

Ariste intercedes with his brother on behalf of Clitandre for the hand of Henriette. Although Chrysale shows himself somewhat sympathetic to Clitandre, Bélise appears and confesses mistakenly that Clitandre actually loves her. She claims that Clitandre pretends love to Henriette to hide this real passion of his. When the brothers laugh at this news, she reminds them of other gentlemen who court her. She refuses to accept the explanations that her conclusions are falsely constructed; some of these supposed suitors have been married now. Fortunately, Bélise leaves them alone to their mutual analysis that she is crazy. When Ariste returns to the subject of marriage between Henriette and Clitandre, Chrysale expresses his enthusiasm about the match. He claims that once he has made the acceptance, his wife will likewise give her assent. With some misgivings, Ariste departs.

Martine reports to Chrysale that she has been fired by his wife; he promises to intervene and save her job. However, Philaminte comes upon them is insistent that the girl be discharged, and poor Chrysale, after timidly defending the girl, is compelled to take his wife's side. However, he does insist upon knowing what prompted the firing of Martine; Philaminte shockingly reveals that the girl, after thirty lessons of grammar, used a vulgar and low word. In stressing her attempt to be understood above all, Martine likewise encounters the opposition of Bélise, stunned by such incorrect speech. The three women are extremists: Philaminte and Bélise have no sympathy for the inability of poorly educated people to comprehend the doctrines of "preciosity," and Martine defies any effort to speak better.

After Martine is sent away, Chrysale criticizes Philaminte and Bélise for not appreciating the girl's qualities; after all, she is a competent servant and performs her role in life admirably. When Chrysale is upbraided for his materialism and lack of concern for intellectual values, he attacks his wife and sister. A woman's place is first and foremost in the home as wife, mother and housekeeper; even the servants have become infected by this disease of learning and neglect their duties. He at last attacks Trissotin as the cause of all this misfortune. Bélise will not remain any longer to hear these insults from her brother. When Chrysale brings up the question of Henriette's marriage, Philaminte asserts her rule of the house. She has selected Trissotin as the right husband and will inform Henriette of the decision first. She exits to make the necessary preparations for her plans. Ariste complains to Chrysale about his weak-willed attitude and abandonment of the mastery of the home. Chrysale wants peace and quiet; when he opposes Philaminte, he has to suffer her temper tantrums. Endeavoring to encourage Chrysale, Ariste warns him that he is sacrificing his manhood and his daughter's happiness because of his cowardice. On the surface, Chrysale gathers courage and promises to settle the marriage between Henriette and Clitandre.

ACT III

Philaminte, Armande, and Bélise are gathered together to hear Trissotin recite some new verses of his. Lépine sits in amusement nearby. The women talk in flowery, indirect language; each strives to outdo the others in flattery and pedantry. Henriette is forced to join the group. After the ladies finally decide to be quiet and let him speak, Trissotin reads his poems-dull, meaningless, and vague. The women go into an ecstacy of delight at insipid phrases, such as "whate'er is said, put it aside." The scene is a

parody of the literary circles of Paris and the current vogue for exaggerated literary airs. As Trissotin declaims each line, he is interrupted by flattering comments; only Henriette shows boredom. Afterwards, Philaminte outlines plans for an academy where women will be able to study the sciences and emancipate themselves from the dominance of men. The crowning glory of this academy will consist of language reform; the work of "preciosity" will be carried to its completion in the purification of French.

At this point of complete enthusiasm, Trissotin introduces his learned friend, Vadius, to the learned ladies, Vadius is welcomed with kisses by the women, except Henriette, when Trissotin declares that his friend knows Greek. Trissotin and Vadius praise each other and their writings to the point of disgust; finally, Trissotin urges his comrade to read some lines. After much demonstration of false modesty, Vadius begins to read when he senses that the others begin to accept his first protests of humility. However, Trissotin interrupts to ask if his friend knows of a certain **sonnet**. Vadius knows the **sonnet** and condemns it as worthless; Trissotin admits his authorship of the poem and a quarrel ensues. Attempting to excuse himself, Vadius strives to convey the impression he was misunderstood. He now scorns the **ballad** written by Trissotin, and the two friends begin to insult each other more and more harshly. Vadius stalks away, promising to challenge his former friend by means of "precious" writing.

Philaminte reveals to Henriette that she wants to improve her daughter's mind by having Trissotin as a son-in-law. As usual, Bélise misunderstands; she thinks the marriage proposal is for her and gallantly steps aside in favor of the niece. Henriette refuses to obey her mother; alone with Armande, she wants her sister to marry this man who has similar ideas. Armande does not want to get married and reminds Henriette of obedience to the mother's wishes. Chrysale, Ariste, and Clitandre enter, and the marriage is settled; however, Armande protests that Philaminte's desires are being ignored.

ACT IV

Armande reports to her mother about the marriage plans of Henriette; Philaminte promises to break up this agreement. Clitandre, entering silently, hears Armande destroy his reputation in the daughter's encouragement of the mother's opposition. Unable to stand these insults, Clitandre emerges and engages in debate with Armande. He admits that he first loved her but could not stand her "precious" airs, her efforts to convert him to these ideals, and consequently fell in love with her sister. Armande criticizes him for being concerned only with the physical side of marriage and not the intellectual achievements of a wife. He admits that he cannot separate body and mind in his concept of marriage. Armande consents to the carnal bond in a possible union with Clitandre, but he is now only in love with Henriette. When the mother intervenes, he pleads with her not to destroy Henriette's happiness by marrying her to such a mediocre writer and ridiculous figure.

Trissotin joins the verbal duel and attacks Clitandre for his ignorance. Much of the argument revolves about the concept of a fool, in other words, a man whom learning does not improve and worsens instead. Trissotin states that the Court of Louis XIV, to which Clitandre belongs, fails to appreciate "preciosity." Clitandre counters that the king's circle should not be expected to yield to the pretentious and boastful claims of a group who live on their own flattery. At this critical point, Julien the valet of Vadius, presents a note from his master to Philaminte. Trissotin is accused of plagiarism and coveting wealth as the reason for marriage with Henriette. However, Philaminte reacts against Vadius: she announces that Trissotin and Henriette will be wed this very evening. Armande and Clitandre challenge each other as to the success of their respective plans; Clitandre hastens to Chrysale for help in thwarting the efforts of Philaminte. Chrysale exits to prepare the marriage of Henriette and Clitandre; the two lovers promise that they will wed no other.

ACT V

Henriette appeals to Trissotin to renounce any claims of marriage on her; she states firmly that she can only love Clitandre. Trissotin apparently loves her and refuses to give up marrying her tonight. Chrysale comes in and shows his defiance of his wife by bringing back Martine; Henriette begs him not to yield when pressure from Philaminte is exerted. Philaminte and the notary argue about the wording of the marriage contract; the former wants it in "precious" language and the latter in the normal, legal form, Philaminte and Chrysale both claim rights to name the husband before the notary; Martine supports the faltering Chrysale. The quarrel is centered on this problem: does the father or the mother have the ultimate decision in family matters? In this particular case, the choice of a husband for a daughter is at stake. Philaminte proposes that Clitandre marry Armande, and Chrysale, to escape from his wife's anger, consents. However, Ariste comes to the rescue. He bears two letters, one to Philaminte and the other to Chrysale. Both communications state that the husband and wife have lost their fortunes through lawsuits and bad investments. Trissotin now refuses the marriage with Henriette since he will have to support the penniless family. His reversal of feelings is so apparent that Philaminte realizes how duped she has been by his insincerity.

Clitandre offers his hand to Henriette. Philaminte accepts the offer; but Henriette, to prove her true love, now refuses to accept because of her poverty. Then, Ariste explains the trick: he has deliberately brought false news to prove that Philaminte had been a fool. To the sorrow of Armande, who wanted Clitandre, and to the usual misunderstanding of Bélise, who believes he still loves her, the marriage contract between Henriette and Clitandre is drawn up.

Comment

First of all, the similarity of *The Learned Ladies* (Les Femmes Savantes) in verse to *The Precious Damsels* (Les Précieuses Ridicules), Molière's prose hit of 1659, must be stressed. In both plays, there is a masculine reaction against the feminist ambitions of wives and daughters; and in both endings, the women are shown the follies of their ways in abandoning so totally their traditional duties. The two comedies condemn not "preciosity" in itself but rather the excesses and exaggerations of the movement and its followers. In the years between 1659 and 1672, Molière had perfected his dramatic talent so that he could criticize, in the second play, the scientific ambitions of these ladies. In the first play, he contented himself with a critique about their use of language; in the second play, Molière chastised their ideals which defied reason, good sense, and moderation. Only in so far as these qualities were omitted by the "learned ladies" and the "precious" women did Molière make fun of them.

In dramatic form, the comedies of 1659 and 1672 show Molière to have developed greatly within these thirteen years. Although a success, *The Precious Damsels* lacks the depth of thought and forceful interest of *The Learned Ladies*; for example, the former is a one-act play and the other is in five acts. The first drama shows traces of the farce and uses broad humor to achieve its aim; the second play is more subtly woven. In other words, the early production stresses action, and the second emphasizes the intellectual theater. There is no real character development in the earlier drama, and in the later offering, Molière has achieved the apex of high comedy, in the conflict of opposing characters. The language is more polished and dialectic in *The Learned Ladies*. The solution of the plot is not known until the appearance of Ariste with the letters; in *The Precious Damsels*, the audience is aware immediately of the disguises of the servants.

There is also, in *The Learned Ladies*, the **exposition** of philosophy of Molière about middle class life; it is a philosophy never formalized but gleaned from repulsion for the extremes. He has an idea of social balance based on the solid virtues of that rising class in France, the bourgeoisie. The middle class virtues of enjoyment of life, sound marriages, and no radical excursions into foreign areas of thought, are cleverly expounded by Molière to offset the exotic appeal of the "precious" and "learned" society groups then flourishing. At the same time, this attitude of Molière has been criticized as fostering conformity against innovation. Again, one must bear in mind that Molière seeks the golden mean between opposites; apparently, he found this solution in the stable traits of the middle class citizens. It must be recalled anew that he wrote and acted for a theater whose financial rewards rested upon acceptance by this class. Above all, he has sketched the concepts and ideals of the backbone of the nation.

THE LEARNED LADIES

CHARACTER ANALYSES

CHRYSALE AND PHILAMINTE

The struggle of character against character which is the essence of high comedy is best illustrated in this play by the husband and wife. In most plays of Molière, the father is the lord of his home, and the mother is at his mercy in all situations. In *The Would-Be Gentleman*, a reaction is noted in the assertions of Mrs. Jourdain; and in *The Learned Ladies*, a complete reversal of roles occurs. Philaminte completely overshadows her husband, and even at the play's end, he has not fully regained his stature despite Philaminte's humiliating experience with Trissotin. However, there remains this basic similarity: no matter who rules within the home, the children are bound to obedience of the parent's wishes. There is also the contrast in the basic attitudes towards life of husband and wife. Chrysale, wishing peace and quiet, is content with enjoyment of the pleasures of his middle class world. Of course, he is also weak-willed and basically conservative; he will admit of no change since present circumstances please him as they are. Philaminte advocates in her literary interests the intellectual pursuits of a household; she wants to reform the way the servants speak, for example.

Thus, curiously enough, the two spouses are opposed on all grounds: intellectual, temperamental, and philosophical. Again, the meaning of Molière, and certainly the meaning is implied and never stated openly, is that the solution must be one of compromise. His sympathies are overwhelmingly on the side of Chrysale, but the reader can also see some justification in Philaminte's aspirations, however wrong her methods may be.

ARMANDE AND HENRIETTE

This clash of characters is revealed from the outset of the comedy; and yet, as Henriette replies in the first act, both girls have the characteristics of their mother. Armande is the purely intellectual woman who seeks in marriage a companion of the soul and who scorns any foundation for a union in sex. For this reason, she rejected Clitandre although it is very evident that she wanted him as a husband. In the fourth act, she offered to accept marriage on his terms but was in turn rejected by Clitandre. Even at the play's conclusion, she feels herself sacrificed for Henriette's love. While one may sympathize with Armande's legitimate wishes to improve her mind, one cannot justify her efforts to destroy her sister's happiness. Her aspirations and ideals have fallen on the battlefield of love and moderation as seen in Henriette. Henriette, even in the obvious contrast in manners of speech, is opposed in personality to her sister. Henriette has no other ambitions than to be a faithful wife and good housekeeper. She represents the other fundamental side of a woman's role in life; it is the traditional attitude against which the "precious" and "learned" ladies of the day were fighting. Again, as in the contrasting views of Chrysale and Philaminte, Molière is on the side of Henriette. Armande has been extreme in the expression of undoubtedly worthwhile desires and aims.

ARISTE AND BÉLISE

Chrysale's brother and sister, although they are relegated to minor parts in the play, are sharply contrasted. Bélise, proclaiming the ideals of the "learned ladies" in speech and behavior, is completely removed from reality and lives in the world of her own thoughts. She misinterprets all the events of the drama and is considered eccentric by Chrysale and Ariste; they avoid and ignore her as much as possible although she is a member of Philaminte's circle of friends. Ariste provides encouragement to Chrysale in his advocacy of a return to male supremacy in the household; he likewise provides the solution to the play's problem and outwits Trissotin at the signing of the marriage contract.

TRISSOTIN AND VADIUS

In this particular instance, both men complement each other in the ridiculousness and fraudulent nature of the prevailing pedantic and literary trends of the Age of Louis XIV. Molière has absolutely no sympathy for the two of them and sharply reveals them as dishonest and hypocritical. His viewpoints are clarified throughout the speeches of Trissotin and Vadius; their language is highly exaggerated and destroys what is of permanent value in the attempt to refine the French language. Of course, the opposition of Chrysale, Clitandre, etc., lends weight to this ponderous attack of Molière. Molière unveils their true natures in the crude language they revert to when they disagree about each other's poems; the snide use of a letter by Vadius to unmask Trissotin; and the latter's undoing when he refuses to marry the apparently impoverished Henriette.

CLITANDRE

Although he clashes in character with Philaminte, Armande, and the pedants, in several ways, he stands apart because he represents the court circles which did not accept the doctrines of the literary salons or drawing-room circles of Paris. Trissotin makes that accusation at him in the fourth act, and Clitandre admits it with pride; Philaminte accuses him of symbolizing the typical noble attitude towards their ideals, which he likewise does not challenge. Thus, in Clitandre, Molière was depicting the man guided by love and moderate ambitions who triumphs in the end by winning the girl. He is certainly the only character who can defy the pedants on their own grounds: the use of polite but forceful language with sound reasoning as the basis for debate.

MARTINE

Like Clitandre, she challenges the rule of the pedants and the "learned ladies," but this servant is an example of stubborn opposition to any linguistic and literary improvement. She defies the others to make her speak better. One cannot defend Martine completely, therefore; she represents the great problem for such reforms as the others advocate, that is to say, the difficulties of educating the masses. She is the typical stock character in Molière's plays: the saucy, outspoken servant who is more realistic than her better-educated superiors and who can help solve the troubles of the lovers.

THE LEARNED LADIES

ESSAY QUESTIONS AND ANSWERS

Question: Discuss the subject of the education of women in *The Learned Ladies*.

Answer: Molière is evidently opposed to the narrow and isolated education of women in convents and private schools; he does not favor complete docility on the part of daughters and wives. Daughters have a right to assert themselves in a choice of husband; wives are to be consulted about family decisions by the husbands. Obviously opposed to the tyranny of husband and father, Molière is an advocate of greater liberty and more breadth of opportunity for women. Never does he wish them to be willing slaves of the masculine will.

However, Molière lashes out in this play against women who abandon their natural inclinations as wife and mother. A woman's place is in the home, Molière would probably assert. When a woman ceases her prime function within the home, she destroys the basis of a happy life for herself and for the family. Henriette is the ideal of feminine education for Molière: she expresses her own feelings about marriage to the man of her choice, Clitandre; at the same time, she does not want to break the traditional bonds of a woman's attachment to the family. To take what is good from the new ideals while adhering to the proven, true, and tried, would be Molière's theory of the education of women. These thoughts may seem very conservative to the contemporary reader, but Molière was attacked by his own contemporaries for the advocacy of liberty and freer education for women. One must keep in mind the historical background of seventeenth century France.

Thus, Molière has chosen a middle path between the two poles of opposite educational theories for women. Against a narrow and slavish upbringing, he also opposes the intellectual pretensions of women who forget their natural inclinations. Women are not constitutionally formed for the literary and social circles he sketches in *The Learned Ladies*. Women who follow such ideas destroy their own happiness and that of their families. Armande is the clear example of this folly in the comedy; she has lost Clitandre because of her "precious" and "learned" ways. Nature has intended women for a role in life and society; it is not the path of competition in a man's world. When man and woman follow their natural instincts and live accordingly, they will be leading happy and useful lives. Women should have the education which fits them for their natural and felicitous part in life and society.

Question: What is the importance of language in *The Learned Ladies*?

Answer: Language replaces money as the basis of a social group.

In his comedies about the middle class, such as *The Miser* and *The Would-Be Gentleman*, Molière demonstrated the power and force of money as the basis of a new class in society. Here, he deals with members of the noble and literary circles of

France who are unconcerned about finances; money plays no role in the play. Language is their main problem; their energies are devoted to the reform and improvement of speech. The most important proof of their removal from reality by the undue stress on speech is found in the scene when Martine is fired for violating so many grammatical rules. It is also ironic that Martine in the most efficient servant in the household; she does her chores seriously and correctly but she refuses to read books and speak better. Thus, concepts and abstractions have taken the place of reality for the literary ladies; they even make plans to form an academy of the elite which will rule over the cultural activities of the nation.

Another characteristic of language in the play is its excessive verbalism. None of the "learned ladies" makes short speeches, and none of them speaks directly. However, the ideas, although clothed in beautiful and complicated linguistic patterns, are not profound; on the contrary, the opinions expressed are always banal. For example, the poetry of Trissotin, incomprehensible in its **syntax**, is devoid of any lofty thoughts or deep observations. Here then on the part of Molière is a commentary upon a contemporary cultural phenomenon made through a device of dramatic **irony**. It is another illustration of the problem of reality and appearance in Molière.

THE PHYSICIAN IN SPITE OF HIMSELF

THE PLAY

CHARACTERS

Sganarelle Martine, his wife Robert, neighbor Géronte Lucinde, his daughter Léandre, Lucinde's suitor Valère, Géronte's steward Lucas, peasant Jacqueline, his wife Thibaut, peasant Perrin, his son

SETTING

Sganarelle's house; Géronte's house.

ACT I

Sganarelle and Martine are arguing heatedly; each complains about the other's faults, and each regrets the day that the words "I do" were pronounced. Sganarelle brags about his experience working for a doctor for six years. Thus he considers himself better educated than his wife. However, Martine fears approaching poverty; Sganarelle is squandering what little income they have on gambling and drinking. She appeals to him for the sake of the hungry four children, but he laughingly dismisses her worries. Her insults begin to irritate him, and he threatens to hit her. After listening to increasingly insulting names, Sganarelle seizes a club and only stops hitting Martine, who is screaming wildly, when Robert enters. He tries to stop the fight between Sganarelle and Martine by scolding the husband for such crude measures. However, Martine turns against Robert and takes the part of her spouse, and Sganarelle also threatens him for interfering in his neighbor's business. The result is that Robert is slapped by Martine and clubbed by Sganarelle for his interference in a domestic dispute. He leaves in haste to allow the family battle to continue.

Sganarelle wants to be friendly again with Martine and promises to work hard today in his job as a woodcutter, but Martine vows revenge for the beating when he goes out. Valère and Lucas approach and discuss the problem of Lucinde, their master's daughter. She has suddenly lost her ability to talk, and Géronte wants her cured so that she can be married to a wealthy suitor, Horace. Another issue in the situation is that she loves someone else, Léandre. However, Valère and Lucas are eager to find medical help for Lucinde because Géronte will then reward them handsomely. After hearing this story, Martine realizes that she can get vengeance on Sganarelle through these strangers. She says that the woodcutter nearby is an excellent doctor even though he may not look the part. The only difficulty is that he is reluctant to demonstrate his medical prowess and has to be coaxed; in fact, according to Martine, he must be clubbed and then he can cure all diseases. Valère and Lucas hasten off in search of Sganarelle and find him without much delay; Sganarelle is sitting peacefully under a tree and is drinking instead of working. He is immediately suspicious of these two unknown figures who eye him up and down and start to question him. When he refuses to admit he is a famous physician after their sly questioning, they change tactics and beat him with sticks.

In order to avoid more beatings, Sganarelle decides to agree to whatever they want; indeed, he ponders upon whether or not he may be able to practice as a doctor. Valère and Lucas encourage him with the promise of whatever fee he may ask. From a humble woodcutter, Sganarelle is transformed, or transforms himself, into an important person; he takes charge of the group and all set upon the road for the trip to Géronte's house.

ACT II

Valère and Lucas brag to Géronte about the marvelous physician whom they have found to cure Lucinde. Although not completely convinced. Géronte consents to see him. While they prepare Sganarelle for his meeting, Jacqueline tells Géronte that the best thing he can do for his daughter is to find her a husband whom she will love. Jacqueline asks Géronte why he did not allow her to have Léandre as a husband; he will be rich one day from the inheritance of an uncle. In Géronte's opinion, money in hand is worth far more than expectations of being heir. Lucas attempts to silence Jacqueline, who insists that happiness and a good husband are the prime requisites of life. Finally, Géronte has to mediate between the husband and wife who begin to quarrel.

Sganarelle, accompanied by Valère, appears for the interview with Géronte; he is dressed in black with a high hat as the physicians were accustomed to do. Still reluctant and fearful to play the part of a learned doctor, Sganarelle has to be struck with a stick by Valère to restore his courage. All these strange actions make Géronte very suspicious and he thinks that Sganarelle is crazy. Sganarelle, enjoying his part more and more, adopts a very formal and learned manner with Géronte. The **irony** is apparent and highly laughable; the more pedantic, boastful, and lying Sganarelle shows himself, the more impressed Géronte becomes at the doctor's wisdom and knowledge. So enthusiastic is Géronte that he runs to get Lucinde for consultation and examination. At this time, Sganarelle notices Jacqueline and starts to flirt with her. Lucas objects but Sganarelle is so clever in his new disguise as a doctor that he is able to outtalk and outwit the poor peasant. Only the reappearance of Géronte with news that Lucinde is coming prevents trouble between Sganarelle and Lucas. However, Sganarelle still has designs on Jacqueline, to Lucas' dismay and fear.

When Lucinde enters, Sganarelle immediately praises her beauty and to the surprise of Géronte, achieves his first victory: he makes her laugh. Nevertheless, Lucinde only utters grunts and groans so that Sganarelle is forced to conduct a humorous inquiry about her health. The impatience of Géronte annoys and confuses Sganarelle; he quotes Aristotle and seeks to be profound to little avail until he discovers that Géronte knows no Latin. Seizing upon this escape device, Sganarelle speaks in a meaningless Latin and describes medical procedures and terminology to Géronte's complete consternation. Toward the conclusion of the diagnosis, Géronte realizes that the doctor has confused the position of the heart and liver. According to Sganarelle, this is due to a new method in medicine.

Sganarelle's remedy is a diet of bread and wine, and Lucinde exists with Lucas. Sganarelle makes passes at Jacqueline by suggesting remedies for her health. Géronte criticizes the medical practices of the day, such as bleeding, but Sganarelle argues learnedly on the subject of preventive medicine. At last, Jacqueline can stand no more and leaves. Géronte wants Sganarelle to accept money, and the latter feigns not to be interested in fees. Nevertheless, when Géronte is insistent, he examines the coins closely to determine if they are genuine. After Géronte departs, Sganarelle ponders about his new career, obviously elated at the thought of earning a great deal of money for nonsensical medical advice. Léandre enters and implores his help in winning Lucinde against her father's opposition. Highly indignant at this insults Léandre until the young man hands him a purse of money. He then changes his attitude and becomes an accomplice of Léandre. Léandre explains that the dumbness of Lucinde is only pretended to prevent marriage to a rival. Sganarelle and Léandre decided to plot for the union of the lovers.

ACT III

Léandre and Sganarelle plot their course of action. Léandre, dressed as an apothecary or doctor's assistant, is timid about his role and asks Sganarelle how he should behave. This makes Sganarelle laugh, since it would be an example of the blind leading the blind. In a very bitter but funny speech, he confesses his complete lack of preparation as a doctor. At the same time, he admits that his early success may induce him to continue this career. After all, doctors are always paid, and if he makes a mistake, the corpse can hardly complain. Two country bumpkins stop Sganarelle for advice for the ailing mother of one of them. Sganarelle is bored with their woes and refuses help until one gives him some money. At sight of a fee, Sganarelle counsels them to give her a particular cheese with certain ingredients. His parting advice is that they should give her a proper funeral if the remedy fails.

Upon entering Géronte's house, Sganarelle again seeks to flirt with Jacqueline. When no success is apparent with flattery, he criticizes Lucas and pities Jacqueline for wasting her qualities on such a husband. These tactics win Jacqueline over, but Lucas has drawn near the two without his presence being known. When they are finally aware of Lucas, they flee and Géronte comes up to the enraged husband. Lucas is sent to fetch Lucinde. Sganarelle and Léandre come to discuss with Géronte the illness of Lucinde, and the suspicious father fails to recognize Léandre, disguised as an apothecary. Lucinde is brought in by Jacqueline, and the two lovers talk on one side of the stage, while Sganarelle blocks Géronte's view by maneuvers and conversation face to face. However, Géronte hears Lucinde speak and now believes her cured. She defies her father on the question of marriage; she will only accept Léandre as her husband.

Géronte notes her state of mind as insane and begs Sganarelle to cure her again. He tells Léandre to escape with her quickly to the garden; all his advice has been given in medical terms so that Géronte thinks she is to be given medicine by Léandre. After they go, Géronte confides in Sganarelle about his many precautions to prevent Léandre from approaching her. Sganarelle mockingly praises his cleverness. Lucas rushes in with the news that the apothecary is Léandre; Léandre and Lucinde have eloped; and Sganarelle is the cause of the trouble. Géronte goes for the police to have Sganarelle arrested, and Martine appears to make fun of her unfortunate husband. However, Géronte comes back and is greeted by the returned Léandre and Lucinde. Léandre has received his inheritance and wants to marry the girl under happy circumstances, that is to say, with the father's consent. This approval is readily forthcoming since the young man has money. Martine claims credit for Sganarelle's success, but he counsels her to take care, treat him with more respect, and beware of a doctor's temper.

Comment

Molière presented in prose *The Physician in Spite of Himself* (*Le Médecin Malgré Lui*) the same year that he offered *The Misanthrope* in verse. Thus, within a few months, Molière performed his most serious and philosophical drama, and certainly one of the most humorous, if not the funniest, plays in his theater. Indeed, *The Physician in Spite of Himself* is not a comedy but a farce. The American critic, Brander Matthews, has spoken of it as having "a Rabelaisian sweep of humor and a Rabelaisian freedom of phrase." Rabelais was the French novelist of the sixteenth century who used earthy humor and uninhibited nature in his writings. This play of Molière has no great lesson to expound nor does it lash out of some defect or social group. Its aim is simply to give pleasure and make the audience roar with laughter. Probably Molière had to gain the favor of his Parisian audiences again after *The Misanthrope* and therefore composed a play more farcical than any previous offering. One should also associate this play with *The Imaginary Invalid*, Molière's last play, because of the low opinions expressed about doctors and medical practices. Molière was suffering more and more from ill health and had himself fallen prey to the doctors. Actually, it has been asserted with much reason that *The Physician in Spite of Himself* would form a worthy sequel to *The Imaginary Invalid*, particularly if the former play were entitled with justification, The Imaginary Physician.

Since it is universally accepted that Molière intended to write an exceedingly comical and farcical play, it is interesting to note how he constructed the play to suit his purposes. Surprisingly, the play, for all its intent at broad comic relief after *The Misanthrope*, is well constructed and logical in its premises. There is a definite rhythm of cause and effect in the drama; for example, the cause for Sganarelle's plight is the beating he administered his wife, and the effect of beatings on him is the exercise of unsuspected medical talents. If the reader also bears in mind the attitude towards doctors and medicine in seventeenth-century France, the effects are not too stupendous. Although the humor is broad and farcical, it is likewise founded on the common and logical device of mistaken identity. Proof that the plot is not too far-fetched can be observed in the overwhelming popularity of this comedy in France and abroad. All in all, the brevity of the play aids in maintaining the dynamic quality of the story; the plot is likewise simple and uncomplicated. There are no subtleties in any of the characters and no complex motives to be analyzed.

Thus the social commentaries are so suppressed as to be almost overlooked, and certainly they were not Molière's aim in *The Physician in Spite of Himself*. Besides the **satire** on medics and medicine, there are the relationships between husband and wife, parents and children, master and servant, and the perennial problem in Molière of marriage.

THE PHYSICIAN IN SPITE OF HIMSELF

CHARACTER ANALYSES

SGANARELLE

There is nothing profound or philosophical in the characterization of Sganarelle. He is the affirmation of life; he loves pleasure and dislikes work, and cannot come to serious grips with money problems and worries about the future. It is clear at the play's beginning that he is not a very good husband and father; he is not above beating his wife and neglecting the children. However, when he is given the chance to play a role in society, as a doctor, he too can demonstrate illusions of grandeur. He is hardly an admirable type, and even at the conclusion, it is seen how he will dominate his wife, seeking his own enjoyment and enrichment. Nevertheless, one is unable to look too askance at him; he is so comical and farcical in action and speech.

MARTINE

Although she is undoubtedly the long-suffering wife, Martine is certainly no model of the perfect mate. She is nagging, quarrelsome, and is not above revenge and jealousy against her husband despite his faults. She is likewise self-centered; for example, she tries to become more pleasant when Sganarelle escapes from the plot against Géronte with success. There are critics who see in the dialogue between Sganarelle and Martine, the reflection of the domestic storms that Molière and Armande Béjart were encountering. At any rate, the argumentative nature of the lines between husband and wife illustrates forcefully the tensions and rising hatreds between spouses. Even if not taken directly from experience, the speeches do indeed show a penetrating comprehension of marital troubles.

GÉRONTE, LUCINDE, LÉANDRE

Géronte is the typical middle class father in so many of Molière's plays. His main interest in life is money, and his principles, if any, follow in pursuit of finances. He was generous in paying Sganarelle only because he saw in his daughter's health the chance for marriage to a rich suitor. When he accepts Léandre so suddenly, Géronte is dazzled by the young man's new inheritance. Lucinde and Léandre are likewise stock characters in Molière's theater: the two young lovers - thwarted by parental opposition. They actually appear at little length in the drama and have minor lines.

ROBERT, VALÈRE, LUCAS, JACQUELINE

The characters from the lower classes of society speak a very frank, even crude, language on the stage, more noticeably than in other productions of Molière. They are not well defined in characterization and are only sketched for the comical aspects involved. Lucas and Jacqueline are examples of marital feuding again although they are not as sharply and bitterly drawn as are Sganarelle and Martine.

THE PHYSICIAN IN SPITE OF HIMSELF

ESSAY QUESTIONS AND ANSWERS

Question: Discuss the attitude of Molière towards doctors and medicine in *The Physician in Spite of Himself*.

Answer: It is necessary to remember that Molière's health was in decline at this time and that he knew from personal experience the problems brought forth in the play. For the modern reader of Molière, the descriptions of the varied aspects of the medical profession may seem exaggerated and only farcical. However, all accounts of medicine and physicians during Molière's lifetime will confirm the shocking and frightening incidents he utilizes. Little if any sound diagnosis was followed; Latin sources were quoted for authority; and Aristotle, the Greek philosopher, was a prime reference. Purges and enemas, as Molière notes, were the favorite treatments, and one can well wonder how any patients survived.

Molière bitterly attacks doctors as fakes and ignorant men who disguise their lack of knowledge under a veneer of learned words and mumbo-jumbo. While Sganarelle is obviously meant to **parody** the poor preparation of doctors, his situation is not so extreme. An ignorant man pretending to be a physician is no more dangerous than charlatans and frauds with antiquated knowledge trying to cheat people out of their money because of their fear of death from illness. However, Molière also reserves criticism for patients, probably including himself, for being such gullible victims of the doctors. Everyone willingly accepts the entrance of Sganarelle into Géronte's house and no one questions his report on Lucinde and his prescriptions. Of course, the critique has great application to the France of Louis XIV, but the fact that audiences have laughed so heartily to the present day may prove that both patients and doctors should exercise great care and caution. At any rate, both groups should get a laugh at each other; Molière would certainly affirm that fact.

Question: *The Physician in Spite of Himself* is probably the best example of an early farce by Molière. Prove this statement.

Answer: Gustave Lanson called great attention in the early twentieth century to the farcical quality of Molière's theater which was derived from medieval French sources. There are constant clubbings of Sganarelle by Valère and Lucas; a brawl between Sganarelle and Martine is part of the first act; Géronte is roughly handled by Sganarelle as a doctor; and the hero is almost killed for supposedly kidnapping Lucinde. There are broad allusions to sex, drinking, and general debauchery throughout the play. The entire tone is one of earthy vitality and enthusiasm for the pleasures of life. There is little reference to morality of fine manners. The primitive instincts, such as revenge, anger, and greed, are major elements in the unfolding of the plot. For example, the prescriptions of Sganarelle for the dying woman, the desire for a fee, and the warning about preparing the funeral, are farcical qualities with social applications.

THE IMAGINARY INVALID

THE PLAY

CHARACTERS

Argan, the imaginary invalid Béline, Argan's wife Angélique, Argan's daughter Louison, younger daughter Béralde, Argan's brother Cléante, Angélique's suitor Mr. Diafoirus, doctor Thomas Diafoirus, his son Mr. Purgon, Argan's doctor Mr. Fleurant, apothecary Mr. Bonnefoy, notary Toinette, servant

SETTING

The home of Argan in Paris.

ACT I

Argan is counting up the cost of the medicines, cathartics, and enemas he has been given by his doctors. He feels that he is not as well this month as last because only twelve enemas instead of twenty have been administered to him. However, he realizes that these physicians are overcharging him; he corrects the bills and is suspicious of the costs of medical care. He soon tires of the accounts and rings impatiently for Toinette to remove the table. Toinette takes her time about arriving, is impertinent with her master, and ridicules the treatments of the doctors, Fleurant and Purgon. She warns Argan that he is only a foil for doctors and that they are using him to collect big fees. Argan sends for Angélique. While he goes out of the room for a while, Angélique and Toinette talk about the former's love for Cléante. There is hope for a marriage since Cléante wrote that he intends asking her hand from Argan. Upon Argan's return, the subject of marriage is brought up; unfortunately for Angélique but comically for the audience, the father and daughter do not have the same man in mind. While Angélique thinks her father is referring to Cléante, Argan has promised her to Thomas Diafoirus, son of his doctor, Diafoirus, and nephew of the other physician, Purgon. When Toinette objects about the match, Argan explains that he wants to have relatives in the medical profession to care for his health. First of all, Toinette does not accept the fact that Argan is ill; if, however, he claims to be ill, why should his daughter, in good health, have to marry a physician?

A bitter argument takes place, curiously enough, between the master and servant about the fate of Angélique. Argan also advocates the match because of the good income of the doctors with whom he will be related. Angélique owes obedience to her father and to consideration of his interests and health. However, Toinette counterclaims by reminding him that Angélique will never give her consent; surely the father will not have the heart to put her into a convent because she is unable to marry a man she does not love. Angered by the repeated criticisms of Toinette, Argan loses his temper and starts chasing her to beat her. According to him, no servant has the right to discuss and criticize the master's affairs; on the contrary, replies Toinette, she has the duty to correct him when he is wrong. Also, she is seeking to prevent him from becoming a fool. Toinette wins, and Argan has to return to his chair, exhausted. Béline comes in and tries to calm her husband down; she arranges his pillows and treats him like an invalid. At the same time, she protects Toinette and reminds Argan that good servants are difficult to find and even more difficult to keep.

Béline, Argan's second wife, is interested in having a will made out; she has brought a lawyer with her to attend to that important business at once. In a sarcastic and sharp attack on lawyers and the vagaries of law, the point is developed that Argan must bequeath his estate now to an intimate so that his second wife will be able to obtain it after his death. This is the only way in which the claims of children can be avoided in the courts. It is obvious from the continuing dialogue that Béline is encouraging Argan in his imaginary illnesses and that she is interested in getting as much money as possible from him. Argan is completely deceived and the three withdraw to another room to prepare the will. Toinette warns Angélique that her stepmother is not to be trusted; the daughter is in danger of losing all claims on her father's wealth. Angélique only wants to marry Cléante; she is uninterested in money. However, Toinette plans to thwart Béline's designs; she will pretend to be on the side of Argan and Béline in order to learn their intentions.

ACT II

Cléante beseeches Toinette for news of Angélique; he is warned by the servant about the increasing difficulty of avoiding the marriage desired by Argan. When the father enters, Cléante introduces himself as the friend of Angélique's singing master who will conduct the lessons for a few days. Toinette endeavors to win Argan's confidence and at the same time restore his faith in his own health by humorous references to his health. Cléante fails to gain admittance to Angélique's room; instead, the girl is brought to him and he will have to give the singing lessons in front of Argan. However, Diafoirus and his son arrive to pay a visit to the patient. The two fathers exchange ceremonious, lengthy greetings, and finally Thomas is introduced. He is the epitome of a clumsy, stupid individual who learns by rote and is lacking in any imagination. He recites an obviously well-rehearsed greeting to Argan; he mistakes Angélique for Béline. Diafoirus explains frankly to Argan that his son is not brilliant and imaginative; in fact, he started to learn to read at the age of nine. However, the father defends the child as loyal and obedient; Thomas is faithful to the classics and has refused to accept any of the new theories, such as the circulation of the blood. Thus he will be a reliable husband for Angélique and a competent physician for Argan, according to Diafoirus Senior. Thomas present a thesis against new medical ideas to Angélique; he also offers to take her to a dissection. As a final convincing argument about the worth of Thomas, Diafoirus assures Argan that he will be able to have many children. When Argan inquires about the possibility of a court position as doctor for Thomas, his father replies that it is better to treat ordinary people; the important people demand that the physicians cure them and are too exacting.

Cléante is told by Argan to have Angélique sing. To conceal his disguise as a singing master, Cléante states that he will direct the performance and that Argan will have a part in the choir. Cléante also explains that he will only sing sections to be understood. In a long narrative in prose, Cléante relates the love of a shepherd and a shepherdess which parallels the love between himself and Angélique. The object is to convince Argan about the advantages of love as the basis of a happy marriage. After a brief recital, Argan stops and dismisses Cléante; he is not persuaded by the plot, words, or music that the performance is valuable. Béline joins the others; Thomas muffs the lines of his prepared introduction and demonstrates again his stupidity. A quarrelsome scene now occurs: Argan insists that Angélique accept Thomas as her husband; Thomas pledges all his charms to please her; and Angélique refuses to obey her father. The argument soon is centered around Béline and Angélique, and the stepmother wants obedience from children to the parents' desires. Angélique pleads for mercy: if her father cannot allow her to marry the man she wishes, he should at least permit her to refuse one whom she does not love. The girl does not want to wed in order to escape from parental control, as many daughters do; in an open thrust at her stepmother, she says she does want to go from husband to husband, collecting inheritances. Béline is obviously insulted at this reference to her own marriage with Argan; therefore, Angélique promises to withdraw and end the discussion. However, Argan will yield to no compromise: he tells Angélique she will either marry Thomas in four days or be sent to a convent.

After this scene of impending crisis, Argan is examined by Diafoirus and his son, and the doctors in question so contradict his other physician's advice that Argan has suspicions. Nevertheless, they are able to restore their prestige by Latin phrases and supposedly learned analysis of the patient. Béline drops by to warn Argan that a man was in Angélique's room; Louison was also there and should be questioned. When Louison appears, Argan threatens to whip her for concealing the truth; she is so frightened that she has to admit her sister asked her to conceal the truth. Argan starts to punish her anyway, and she feigns death; only then, Argan relents and shows his paternal affection. Realizing that the singing master is trying to make love to Angélique, Argan sends back Louison with instructions to spy on them and inform him. Exhausted, Argan remembers he is supposedly very ill and rests in his chair. Béralde enters to propose a suitor for Angélique, but Argan, infuriated at the mention of his daughter's name, expounds upon his intention to send her to a convent. Trying to calm his brother, Béralde introduces a group of entertainers who will sing and dance for Argan to relax him; in fact, Béralde says frankly that they are better medicine than the prescriptions of the doctors.

ACT III

After the performance, Béralde and Argan begin to talk over some business. However, Argan has to make one of his several hurried exits to the bathroom; these interludes serve the purpose of letting other characters perfect their plots. For instance, Toinette now enters and encourages Béralde to oppose Argan's plans. She herself has a project: she will disguise herself as a physician and come to cure Argan. Toinette vanishes fast when Argan reappears.

The two brothers quarrel about Angélique's future, and Béralde endeavors vainly to warn Argan about Béline's real intentions. Béralde likewise criticizes Argan's self-interest in wanting his children to marry for his own welfare. Under this procedure, Louison will have to wed an apothecary, insists Béralde; and surprisingly, Argan thinks it to be a good idea. As a last resort, Béralde attacks the whole treatment of Argan; Argan must be as strong as an ox or otherwise all the medicines he has taken would have killed him. However, if Argan continues taking all these enemas and purges, he will surely be dead, advises his brother. At this point, an interesting debate ensues about the role of medicines and doctors in society. Béralde believes that so little is known about the human body that the best remedy is to do nothing when ill and let nature heal the illness; he also states that doctors are so incompetent and confused that their function is less than useless-it is dangerous. The doctors are sincere in their ignorance, and in this unfortunate situation resides the tragedy of present medical care. Béralde succinctly summarizes his argument by asserting that medical theory is quite impressive and erudite but has nothing to do with reality. As a concluding thrust, Béralde advocates that the plays of Molière be seen for a witty and accurate commentary on these problems. Molière does not attack the physicians as persons; he criticizes them as misinformed individuals. Molière scorns the cures in vogue and suffers his maladies in silence.

Béralde attempts to return the conversation to Angélique's plight about the forced marriage. However, Fleurant enters with the enema he has prepared for Argan; Béralde urges his brother to stop this treatment which will kill him. For the first time, Argan changes his mind and tells Fleurant to return later. At this defiance, Fleurant promises to inform Purgon about the patient's rebellion; he also ridicules Béralde for preventing the prescriptions of Purgon. Furious at this action against his orders, Purgon enters and warns Argan about the fatal results which this rebellion will have. The doctor also breaks off the agreement of a wedding gift for his nephew, Thomas. He enumerates in medical, meaningless jargon the list of symptoms Argan will begin to suffer; soon his disobedient patient will be dead. Terrified at his approaching fate, Argan blames his brother for it; Béralde seizes this chance to encourage Argan to give up all medicines and doctors. Now is his opportunity to recover; Argan remains unconvinced. Toinette announces that a new physician wants to see Argan, but tells Argan not to be surprised at the marvels of this new doctor. For example, the doctor bears an amazing resemblance to her.

The new doctor is of course Toinette who has to make some fast entrances and exits to fool Argan; she changes disguises during these appearances rapidly so that he will not guess the trick being played on him. A farcical scene ensues in which Toinette completely persuades Argan that the diagnosis of Purgon has been wrong. She replies "the lungs" to each description of a complaint from Argan; she also orders a diet of hearty foods in quantity. As a final insult to the prevailing medical arts, she proclaims that if Argan has one arm and one eye removed, the remaining members will be strengthened by their reception of that surplus energy. Thinking the moment is opportune after Toinette's exit, Béralde returns to the subject of Angélique's marriage, but Argan is as stubborn as previously on this matter. Finally, Béralde comes into the open and accuses Béline of plotting against the interests of Argan and Angélique. Toinette, pretending now as the returned servant to defend Béline and Argan, tricks her master once more. She tells Argan that he can verify how Béline loves him: he will pretend to be dead, Béralde will hide nearby, and the reaction of Béline will be the proof.

The solution comes with Béline's appearance and joy at the sight of the supposedly dead Argan. She heaps scorn upon her husband and tells Toinette to keep the news quiet until she can take some valuable papers and the available money away. However, when she searches Argan for the keys, he gets up and denounces her for the deception she has used on him as a wife. Toinette then urges Argan to play dead again to note Angélique's reaction. Angélique and Cléante both express their true grief at the sight of the rigid Argan; Angélique promises to honor one wish of her father-to enter the convent. When Argan arises, he is reconciled to his daughter and to the choice of Cléante as a husband. However, he wants the young man to become a doctor. Béralde has a better idea: Argan should become a doctor. All convince him that with a beard, cap and gown, and the use of learned words, he will be a success. Béralde will arrange for a company of entertainers to perform the initiation ceremony, and Argan will have a principal part. Argan agrees with some reluctance, and everyone prepares for the evening's festivities.

Comment

Despite the fact that *The Imaginary Invalid* (Le Malade Imaginaire), in prose, is a farce and a musical comedy with its humorous initiation ceremony at the end, there is a morbid and naturalistic quality to the play, uncommon in Molière. The whole **theme** of the power of doctors and their ineptitude is particularly frightening when one reads the contemporary accounts which verify this situation. Nothing less than the control over life and death is involved in the ignorant manipulations and comments of these individuals. At the same time, death is stressed as a basic idea in the play in the pretended demise of Louison from her father's beating, and the reactions of Béline and Angélique before the prone Argan. In sharp contrast to this somber aspect, one sees the very realistic references and comments about Argan's health, his medical diagnosis, and the characteristics of body functions. In these two areas, the play enters a new phase in Molière's theatrical achievement.

This last comedy of Molière is undoubtedly the most subjective he wrote; it is also the most pathetic in many ways. While the comic element is naturalistic and the drama is farcical, there is the undeniable feeling that Molière is expressing his own tragic circumstances in Argan. Perhaps for these reasons, we do not find the brilliance of dialogue, the opposing arguments, and the sharply etched drawings of a middle class society. The plot shifts from the foiling of the doctor's influence over Argan to the outwitting of Béline. One should compare and contrast the two plays, *The Physician in Spite of Himself* and *The Imaginary*

Invalid, to observe the transformations of Molière's art between 1666 and 1673. The former is light comedy; its light humor and comical situations revolving about the trick played on a master lack the sober implications of the second representation. The first drama is less bitter than the second, although the conflicts between husband and wife are sharply emphasized.

THE IMAGINARY INVALID

CHARACTER ANALYSES

ARGAN

The portrait of a hypochondriac seems to have been drawn by Molière from his own unhappy experiences with doctors and his disillusionments with them. One must recall that the fatally ill Molière, playing the part of an imaginary invalid, collapsed and died as a result of his efforts in this play. In the third act, there is the revealing exchange about his own views on the subject of physicians and medicine in the conversation between Béralde and Argan. Argan is not ill physiologically but psychologically: he imagines that he is sick and convinces himself that this is true. Béralde constantly brings out this point. Argan is basically kind and good, as when he relents from punishment of Louison whom he thought he whipped fatally. He is also pitiful in the way his second wife, Béline, exploits him. Being a farce, however, *The Imaginary Invalid* terminates on a happy note for Argan when, as a doctor, he can practice the medical arts to his heart's content.

BÉRALDE

As Argan's brother, he is the ideal counterpart to the oddities and eccentricities of Argan. He is a man who is mildly skeptical, reasonable, and tolerant; he does not attack the physicians on personal grounds but on their inaccurate training. He is on the side of justice and happiness; he aids Angélique and Cléante to win Argan's approval for the marriage. Beyond a doubt, he represents the ideas of Molière on the issue of the medical arts and man's place in the social framework.

BÉLINE

She is one of the cruelest, if not the most vicious, feminine characters in Molière's theater. Her shameless exploitation of her husband's obsession with medicine and doctors is matched only by her shocking comments upon seeing the supposed corpse of Argan. Béline also seeks to destroy the future bliss of Angélique by opposing the marriage with Cléante. Probably for these reasons, Molière chose to dub her the second wife of Argan. She is one of the few personages in the plays for whom no sympathy can be demonstrated.

TOINETTE

As in almost every comedy, the servant provides the key to much of the humor and certainly the solution of the play's problem. Toinette is one of the most vivacious of all the servants in Molière's theater. She has entrances and exits in all the acts of *The Imaginary Invalid*; she prods Argan into rebellion against the medical treatments; and she uses the doctor's disguise to disillusion him at last about his follies.

ANGÉLIQUE AND LOUISON

Louison only appears in one very touching scene, the interview with her father, but this **episode** so impressed Goethe, the German author of Faust, that he called it masterly. Louison, in her childlike manner, brings out the innate humanity and paternal love of Argan. Angélique and Louison are victims of paternal domination and the tyranny of a stepmother. Angélique does challenge Argan and Béline on the question of marriage and is forceful in expressing her own will; she is not as placid as several other daughters in Molière's works.

CLÉANTE

As the young lover, he is surprisingly weaker in his assertions to wed Angélique than other suitors in Molière. Usually, the male will be more prepared than the female to combat the rule of parents for the hand of the loved one. All in all, Cléante is a rather weak character, especially in his bumbling effort to imitate a singing master.

PURGON, FLEURANT, DIAFOIRUS, AND THOMAS DIAFOIRUS

Molière was not satisfied to level a broadside at the medical profession by satirizing one doctor. He has depicted in the drama four members of the trade. Purgon and Fleurant collaborate closely to cheat Argan; for that reason, Argan cannot detect anything wrong in their diagnosis. However, Diafoirus, in league with his relative, Purgon, adds some refinement to the cure of Argan; there are contradictory aspects to his theories. The greatest danger is that the ridiculous teachings of these men will be continued in Thomas; of more consequence, Thomas is completely stupid. Thus, he will not only follow in the path of ignorance of the profession and his family; he will add the ingredients of his own small intelligence and talent.

THE IMAGINARY INVALID

ESSAY QUESTIONS AND ANSWERS

Question: What is Molière's solution for the problem of the medical profession, doctors, and medicine?

Answer: Molière bases his attack upon existing medical practices on two points: ignorance and deceit. In the first case, he does not blame the practitioners of his day for their habits; they know no better. In many cases, they consider themselves upright and humanitarian individuals. They are the victims of a system which admits no wrong; they have been trained not to challenge existing practices. For these men, Molière only has pity and regret that they enjoy such advantages over humanity.

On those who knowingly cheat and betray their patients, Molière heaps great scorn. These members of the medical profession pad their bills, prescribe ridiculous preparations to gain prestige as outstanding doctors, and have no fears about killing the patient. The fraudulent efforts of these men will destroy all confidence in the healing arts and result in the continuation of a vested interest fighting any scientific improvement in the use of medicine. Together, the two groups lead to complete disenchantment in the public. The solution for Molière will be to ignore any device from doctors.

Molière, undoubtedly remembering his personal experiences with doctors, inserts his own name and theories into the play at one point. Nature is the best physician; the natural balance of the person's constitution will cure him. Rest is of the most vital importance. Again, the reader of Molière must not reject Molière's ideas as extreme, although he himself would strenuously deny them; the contemporary scene of three hundred years ago must be kept in mind. Too much reliance, born of evident fear, had been placed on doctors, and they had established themselves so firmly that they refused to change their theories. At the same time, Molière's remedy of rest and proper care are certainly standard procedures in present-day medical therapy. Thus, Molière is an important forerunner in calling attention to one of the outstanding issues of his age.

More skepticism is needed on the part of patients; they should use reason and moderation in judging the advice of physicians. Then, the medical profession will be compelled by a reluctant public to change its ways. It is known that the play had a great success; what exact influence it may have exerted upon changes in medical practice cannot be determined. Even today, the types Molière has described can be enjoyed; he is also drawing contemporary lessons.

CONCLUSIONS

DRAMATIC ART

Molière built upon the solid base of the French farce and the Italian comedy-of-masks, and the main element in his theater is humor. He wanted to please the public and to make them laugh at their own foibles and those of mankind in general. Molière went from low comedy to high comedy in the years between 1659 and 1673; he returned to broad laughter in his last play, *The Imaginary Invalid*. Although his plots are contrived and his endings artificial, he brought the French virtues of reason, moderation, and good sense, then coming to vogue in the Age of Louis XIV, to the comedy. Tragedy was considered the only worthwhile dramatic art of the times, but Molière was able to create a popular theatrical form utilizing the theories of the French classicists. He could range from a comedy of manners, to a comedy of intrigue, to a comedy of character. The laughter invoked by Molière is both general and particular: it has direct application to the France of his day, but a reader can laugh just as heartily today at the vices and defects Molière criticizes.

SOCIAL VISION

Molière is more than a painter of portraits because he draws a fresco of society as a whole, as the French critic of the nineteenth century, Sainte-Beuve, noted. His characters are varied and vivacious. In the most controversial play, Tartuffe, the king himself, while not appearing nevertheless is the personage who saves the family from Tartuffe's machinations. The nobility is brought into many of the comedies: generally the nobles are depicted favorably, but Molière is not adverse to inserting profligate and dishonest members of the aristocracy. Even servants and peasants find a place in his theater and speak a natural, conversational language. Of course, Molière pays most attention to the middle class and concentrates upon their aspirations and problems. Money, social status, marriage, and the careers of children, are some of the issues of the bourgeoisie with which he deals. He also treats the problems, accentuated by the changing social patterns of seventeenth century France, of human relations. The relations between husband and wife, fathers and daughters, and other members of the family are discussed. Lawyers and doctors are also commented upon, usually in a very unfavorable light. Whether or not one accepts the thesis that Molière is deliberately sketching a social vision of his times and outlining the problems of his age, must depend on one's study of the works. The family, based on the rule of harmony, love, and mutual understanding, is the foundation of a happy nation and life; the middle class would seem to express this ideal if one notes the emphasis placed upon its role in Molière's theater.

PHILOSOPHY OF LIFE

Molière's attitudes of conduct for the individual are never definitely spelled out, but the repetitions of certain viewpoints in his sympathetic characters lead to certain conclusions. Molière does not fall into the category of an optimist or a pessimist about human nature. Men are seldom so good or so bad as they appear;

people must be accepted as they are, or to use a modern saying, "people are funny." By following nature and natural instincts, man will probably not go far astray from the path of harmony and cooperation. Extremes in any form are to be avoided, and the radical exponent of virtue or vice can be undone by the placid qualities of reason and moderation. Perhaps there exists the hope for a change to the better in humanity, but Molière is not so sure. Anyway, the positive example set by good sense may achieve some minor improvement. Thus, the philosophy of Molière is practical: tolerance and a smile for poor, suffering mankind beset by foibles, quirks, and life's agonies. The social bond, in the family and in society, holds the individual together.

INFLUENCE

The French have generally praised Molière as their greatest, and certainly most popular, writer because he embodies the traits and virtues they hopefully see in themselves. He has been always studied from the universities to the elementary schools, and the Comédie Française is the living testament to his continuing favor and enduring fame. Fundamentally, the appeal of Molière is popular, a fact which he would have appreciated. Nevertheless, he has exercised an influence over French thought and letters for the past three hundred years, and the annual bibliographies of Molière studies show that his impact is as strong as ever.

For those outside France, the enjoyment of Molière is probably due to the pensive laughter and broad humor which are universal in attraction. Certainly the figures he introduced to the stage have an immediate application beyond the world of Paris under Louis XIV. Goethe summed up this spirit by writing that "Molière is a genuine man; there is nothing distorted about him. He chastened men by drawing them just as they are." In other words, the audience, foreign or French, may observe some readily identifiable elements of their own personalities in the actors. Thus, the two causes for the lasting value and contribution of Molière abroad are the comical backdrop of all the plays and the general resemblance to other existing people and problems.

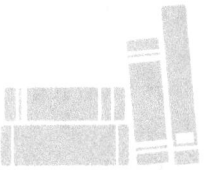

CRITICISM

In the twentieth century, Molière criticism has concentrated on the works rather than on the life of the man. Little is known of Molière and investigation has revealed no great discoveries. In fact, the evidence available was found not to be completely reliable. Consequently, critics have paid more attention to the plays. It has been impossible to write biographies of Molière from psychoanalytical or even existential viewpoints. While the French have obviously led in the field of Molière studies, American academic research has made noteworthy contributions.

EARLY CRITICAL INTEREST, 1900-1925

In 1901, Gustave Lanson, one of the most respected of French critics at that time, sought to define the genius of Molière by asserting that he is basically French in influence and spirit. Lanson claimed that the prime characteristic of Molière is his use of the old French farce. He admits that Molière is weak in the structure of his plots and that Italian and Spanish influences are apparent. However, Molière molded the French farce into great comedy by the depiction of social conditions. Thus, the prime element in Molière is the farcical and laughter from the audience is his aim.

René Jasinski, another major French critic of the century, took an opposite view: he saw in the plays a very personal and heart-rending confession on the part of Molière. He paid particular attention to *The Misanthrope* in which the evolution of a profound and melancholy philosophy by Molière was observed. Jasinski endeavored to strengthen his case by a detailed and scholarly analysis of the historical, social, and literary backgrounds of the times. Despite the variance in views of such critics, Molière was coming to the attention of the public; men such as Lanson and Jasinski helped to show that Molière was not reserved for children and university classes; in other words, the plays were meant to be acted and applied to modern times.

For example, Gustave Michaut published one of the fundamental texts of the plays in the period 1921-1925. To the new emphasis upon the interpretation of the works was now added the necessary text. Michaut also battled with more daring critics of Molière; he preferred a more standard and historical interpretation of the plays. Ramon Fernandez saw in the plays a comedy of will; he even saw in the comic hero of Molière a mockery of the classical French characters of Corneille and Racine, Molière's great contemporaries.

STAGE REVIVALS, 1925-1945

The result of the critical interest and enthusiasm for the performance of Molière's plays was now apparent in the shift from the reading to the viewing. In this area, Louis Jouvet is the outstanding figure; he popularized Molière on the stage and also in writings and speeches. One of the cardinal principles of Louis Jouvet was that Molière cannot be understood outside the theater. The actor is the most important figure in any interpretation of Molière; the scholars and critics have lost sight of this single most important facet of Molière's art. Jouvet followed in the footsteps of Molière to revive the theater: he served as both actor and director of his own theatrical company. He staged the plays in very original and modern form, such as the use of the revolving stage. His production of *The School for Wives* inaugurated the great revival of Molière in 1936, and his company also toured the United States. Jouvet gave bold renditions of the characters: Arnolphe in *The School for Wives* is a man so possessed by the spirit of money that he has acquired a cackling laugh; Tartuffe is a man not quite false who is tempted by the flesh into sin.

René Bray, emphasizing the role of the actor, supported the interpretation of Louis Jouvet. He based his arguments on more scholarly grounds: Molière was strongly influenced by the traditions of the French theater and also the many actors and theatrical groups of his day, particularly Italian. Molière realized the importance of movement and gesture and how to make an audience pay attention not to the words but to the actor. In short, René Bray recalled the theatricality of Molière and explained the dramatist in terms of the stage.

OPPOSITION TO MOLIÈRE

Nevertheless, Molière has not secured a total triumph in the twentieth century; there are still forces which oppose him. For instance, the government of Marshal Pétain in Unoccupied France during 1940-1942 tried to prevent any productions of Tartuffe as too controversial and destructive of morals. François Mauriac, novelist and recent winner of the Nobel Prize in literature, has severely criticized Molière for being antireligious and lacking in love of God. More indirectly, Molière is condemned for his attacks on society and values. One critic, Jacques Audiberti, has compared the genius, achievement, and controversial natures of Molière and Charlie Chaplin.

PRESENT STAGE INTERPRETATIONS

Jacques Copeau and Jean-Louis Barrault, associates of Louis Jouvet, have also transformed the plays of Molière into modern stage productions. Copeau emphasized the farcical aspect of Molière and likewise traced this quality to the Italian influence; he called great attention to the popular nature of Molière's theater. Molière, writing for the people, adopted the popular traits of his day and perfected them. Copeau employed practically an empty stage in his productions in order to emphasize the importance of the actor, the movements, gestures, and speeches of the characters. Barrault has continued this new technique; for example, he staged *The Misanthrope* in a black and white setting. He interpreted Alceste as a young man, immature in his judgments, instead of a mature and embittered individual.

An opposite interpretation of Molière exists: the French National Theater, particularly in its production of *The Would-Be Gentleman*, sought to present a lavish and ornate production with rich costumes and expensive settings such as Louis XIV wanted. The background and the satirical elements are predominant instead of the comical. The viewer is tempted by most stage offerings of the Comédie Française to recall the backgrounds and ringing social criticisms. Of course, the acting is superb, and the two leading actors would seem to be Louis Seigner and Robert Hirsch.

THE "NEW CRITICISM" OF MOLIÈRE

As critics interpreted the plays increasingly in terms of the texts themselves and as performances showed that actors could give a variety of renditions to Molière, the language of the dramatist received more attention. Will G. Moore in 1949 focused upon Molière the techniques of the "New Criticism." According to this literary theory, the life of the writer is practically omitted from any critical consideration and a strict linear reading of the manuscript is sought. For example, Moore studied the speech of Molière with concentration and found that the dialogue had social functions in many respects. Molière used speech not only to be obviously understood but also to be misunderstood, misheard, incomprehensible, and incoherent. There is not the sole aim of the comical, as other critics asserted, but a deeper meaning, according to Moore. Molière was commenting throughout the plays upon the artificial language of his age; this acid reaction of his was missed by critics. Molière's speech is likewise excellent dramatic form, and Moore writes that "the principle at work here is dramatic **irony**. This is used with remarkable consistency throughout Molière's comedy and no definition of his art can fail to include it as an ingredient. The dramatist makes his puppets say what, on reflection, they would not say. All of us are funny when we say what we do not mean, or when our speech, intending to convey definite meaning, conveys something more, or conveys precisely that which we would hide. This does not happen nearly so often in life as in Molière's plays." Moore thus found a unified structure and a highly intellectualized comic spirit in the new critical approach to Molière.

Judd D. Hubert followed the procedure of a close reading of the dramas and traced certain **themes** in individual plays. He found the same unified structure which Moore claimed although by means of these central ideas. Likewise, he omits any biographical considerations unless they are absolutely necessary. One of his conclusions is that Molière deliberately selected comedy as his field; the choice of the theater was not accidental or historical as older, historical critics have insisted. Hubert finds in the complex themes the deep and brooding nature of Molière: for example, Alceste in *The Misanthrope* is a self-deceiver and self-deception is the main quality of the play. Harpagon in *The Miser* represents inhumanity at its worst; he sums up all the evils and vices which can befall a family.

Lionel Gossman continued in the tradition of the "new criticism" as has been observed in Moore and Hubert but tried to view Molière more "in the context of the experience and thought of his age." In other words, Gossman adhered to the new pattern of a close and thorough textual reading without any undue mention of the facts of Molière's life. However, he did interpret the plays as part and parcel of the age of Louis XIV; he also made his interpretations in the light of philosophical thought of the times. For example, he sees in the fall of Tartuffe by the intervention of Louis XIV, the substitution of one idol for another. Thus, according to Gossman. Molière certainly had relevance for the eighteenth century which overthrew the monarchy.

THE ECLECTIC APPROACH TO MOLIÈRE

Alfred Simon believes that the art of Molière is so diversified that no one element stands out. He cannot accept previous theories about the preponderance of the farcical and comical qualities as the outstanding virtues, the idea that Molière is always a serious and profound writer, and that the dramatist always advocated common sense and a simple morality. Simon states that Molière must be viewed in terms of his age; Molière both acted and reacted to the political and social forces at work as well as the theatrical demands of the time. For instance, Simon reads *The Misanthrope* as a political comedy and he calls it "both a peak and a dead end." Molière saw the advantages of royal favor throughout his career and at the same time realized how fragile was the king's protection in the furor about Tartuffe. According to Simon, Molière realized the problems of the age of Louis XIV and accepted the situation so that "since the king and France are one, in creating a royal theater he will give the age its first popular theater." Thus, Molière must be considered in his totality; each play must be viewed in the light of the particular problem involved. In some cases, it may be political; in others, biographical.

Jacques Guicharnaud of Yale University studies in close detail key plays of Molière as illustrating the dramatist's employment of masks; that is to say, there is "a certain **realism** within the unreality." Guicharnaud writes of *The School for Wives* that "the spectator finds himself in both the imaginary and the real, literature and life; he is torn apart, as he should be in the theater-pulled out of himself toward the innocent delights of theatrical illusion and at the same time thrown back on himself to the reality of his basic instincts. He has to deal with the contemptible masks of the traditional stage, but the papiermache of the mask has become flesh, while keeping its original shape and colors. Such transmutation is painful for the audience." Thus, there are two levels of interpretation to the drama being enacted on the stage, the masks of Guicharnaud represent the old literary problem of illusion and reality. The audience knows that a comedy is being performed, laughs at the actions and mishaps, and yet has misgivings that perhaps the spectators are seeing themselves on the stage. This is why Guichardnaud insists that Molière is such an innovator; he is the

Beckett and Ionesco, contemporary avant-garde dramatists of today, of the seventeenth century.

SUMMARY

While the divergence of critical opinion about Molière would seem to preclude any dogmatic assertions about the meanings of the plays, the increasing emphasis upon the full wealth of implications in the dramatist shows that he is not a simple comedian. The differences of opinion and shifts in theories from the early historical and biographical approaches to the "new criticism" concern for the strict textual reading, the concern for structure, and the application of contemporary sociological and philosophical ideas demonstrate the values of Molière today. Molière still has much to say about the present-day world in the average and ordinary sense; he is also very much alive in the interpretations of scholarly critics. For instance, Jacques Audiberti, in his fascinating comparisons of Molière and Charlie Chaplin, writes that "the works of Chaplin and those of Molière grow, from one to the other, under the weight of almost continual good fortune. Farce becomes an ethic, the cream pie a philosophy. The puppets are greeted as monumental champions of a humanity which is no longer obsolete or theoretical but which everyone can touch, there and then."

If the ideas of critics and scholars become too controversial, it is well to recall the popular quality of Molière which no writer denies. Molière dominates the field of the comic theater; all the theoreticians agree to this fact. On the contrary, the wide range of views should be welcomed as proof of the vitality of Molière beyond his age; he is popular in terms of today and yet holds a vast appeal for more erudite circles seeking the myriad qualities of his genius. It is perhaps sufficient to conclude that the bibliographies of Molière will continue to reflect diverse and opposite ideas. This might have caused Molière to laugh-or it might have furnished him with a humorous situation for a play.

BIBLIOGRAPHY

WORKS

The Plays of Jean Baptiste Poquelin Molière, trans. A. R. Waller. Edinburgh: John Grant, 1926. 8 vols. Text in French and English. (Good for comparing original and translation on adjoining pages. The translations are accurate but stilted.)

Eight Plays by Molière, trans. Morris Bishop. New York: Random House, 1957. The Modern Library. (Lively and colloquial translations which reflect Molière's language; sparkling introductions.)

Plays of Molière. New York: Random House, n. d. The Modern Library. (An inexpensive edition of the plays in uninspired translations.)

The Misanthrope, trans. Richard Wilbur. New York: Harcourt, Brace & World, 1955.

Tartuffe, trans. Richard Wilbur. New York: Harcourt, Brace & World, 1963. (The best available translations in style and spirit of Molière.)

CRITICISM

Edelman, Nathan, ed. *The Seventeenth Century* ("Molière," pp. 226-43). Vol. III of A Critical Bibliography of French Literature, ed. David Cabeen and

Jules Brody (Syracuse: Syracuse University Press, 1961). (A list of the outstanding critical articles and books on Molière in French and English.)

Fernandez, Ramon. *Molière: the man seen through the plays*. Trans. Wilson Follett. New York: Hill and Wang, 1958. (A biography of Molière deduced from textual analysis; will is a basic idea in the works.)

Gossman, Lionel. *Men and Masks, a Study of Molière*. Baltimore: The Johns Hopkins Press, 1963. (Intense analysis of the texts which reflect the whole age and thought of the seventeenth century.)

Guicharnaud, Jacques, ed. Molière. *A Collection of Critical Essays*. Englewood Cliffs, N. J.: Prentice-Hall, 1964. (A compendium of popular and scholarly articles of the twentieth century on Molière.)

Hubert, Judd D. *Molière and the Comedy of Intellect*. Berkeley and Los Angeles: University of California Press, 1962. (Concentration upon the texts to deduce basic **themes** in each play.)

Lancaster, Henry Carlington. *"The Period of Molière,"* in *A History of French Dramatic Literature in the Seventeenth Century*, Part III (2nd ed. Baltimore: The Johns Hopkins Press, 1952. (Important for the historical and social background of the times.)

Lanson, Gustave. "Molière and Farce" (trans. Ruby Cohen), Tulane Drama Review, VIII, 2 (Winter 1963), 133-54. (A pioneer study calling attention to traditional French influence on Molière.)

Lewis, Wyndham D. B. *Molière: The Comic Mask*. New York: Coward-McCann, 1959. (Popular biography in an animated personal style.)

Matthews, Brander. *Molière, His Life and His Works*. New York: Scribner's, 1910. (The historical and social approach to the understanding of Molière and his works.)

Moore, Will G. *Molière, A New Criticism*. Oxford: The Clarendon Press, 1949. (A basic book which revolutionized Molière criticism by emphasizing textual study.)

Palmer, John L. *Molière*. New York: Brewer and Warren, 1930. (A compromise between popular biography and the new critical methods.)

Saintonge, Paul, and Robert W. Christ. *Fifty Years of Molière Studies*, a Bibliography, 1892-1941. Baltimore: The Johns Hopkins Press, 1942. (A thorough outline of the fate of Molière in English and French; essential for beginning bibliography.)

_____. "Omissions and Additions to Fifty Years of Molière Studies," Modern Language Notes, LIX (1944), 282, 85. (Updating to the previous study; both lists provide starting point, with Lancaster's work, for Molière criticism.)

www.ingramcontent.com/pod-product-compliance
Lightning Source LLC
LaVergne TN
LVHW021720060526
838200LV00050B/2770